REVOLUTION:
The Story of John Lennon

REVOLUTION: The Story of John Lennon

John Duggleby

MORGAN REYNOLDS

PUBLISHING

Greensboro, North Carolina

REVOLUTION: THE STORY OF JOHN LENNON

Copyright © 2007 by John Duggleby

Library of Congress Cataloging-in-Publication Data

Duggleby, John, 1952-
    Revolution : the story of John Lennon / John Duggleby. -- 1st ed.
        p. cm.
    Includes bibliographical references (p.   ) and index.
    ISBN-13: 978-1-59935-034-9
    ISBN-10: 1-59935-034-3
    1. Lennon, John, 1940-1980. 2. Rock musicians--Biography. I. Title.
    ML420.L38D84 2007
    782.42166092--dc22
    [B]

                                                    2006033855

Printed in the United States of America
First Edition

To Mom and Dad, who endured Beatlemania

Contents

John Lennon 1940–1980

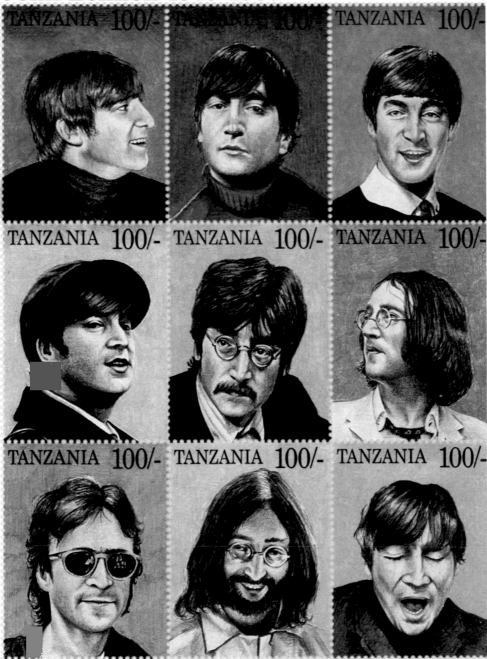

John Lennon Stamps (Courtesy of Associated Press)

War time

The fall of 1940 was a dangerous time in Liverpool, England. It was the darkest days of World War II. France had fallen to the Nazis in June and now only Great Britain held out against the German onslaught. Liverpool was a port city and was crucial to both the British economy and to the navy. German dictator Adolph Hitler had ordered massive air attacks against major British cities and Liverpool was one of the prime targets. Almost every night the shipyards were bombed. Occasionally, the bombs missed their targets and landed in neighborhoods.

One bomb had fallen dangerously close to Oxford Street Maternity Hospital only days before Julia Lennon was admitted. Fortunately, October 9, 1940, the day Julia gave birth to her first child, was quiet. The new mother christened her son John, adding the middle name of Winston in honor of Winston Churchill, the new prime minister who was rallying the British people to resist the Nazis.

John Lennon was born in Liverpool, England, during World War II.

After her son was delivered Julia called her older sister, Mimi Smith, who ran the two miles from her house to the hospital because the bombing raids had grounded the local buses. Mimi, who had no children of her own, mothered the baby from the beginning. "Take this blanket off his face, it's too rough," she ordered when she first saw him. When she returned home, Mimi gushed to John's new grandparents that "the others are all wrinkled and he isn't."

The chaos in young John's family life mirrored the chaos of the outside world. His father, Freddie, was not around. Julia said he was a steward in the navy, but no one knew for sure where he was. Julia and Freddy had lost touch. When he was older John was told that his father was off somewhere fighting the "Nasties." The truth was that Julia and Freddie's casual relationship had collapsed.

They had met when both were about sixteen. Freddie, sporting a bowler hat usually worn by stodgy English businessmen, had given Julia the eye as she sat on a Liverpool park bench. When she saw him staring Julia said, "You look silly."

"You look lovely," he replied. When Julia insisted Freddie remove the hat if he wanted to sit with her and he flipped it into a nearby lake. Julia liked Freddie's spontaneity, which became a hallmark of the courtship that followed.

Freddie was a born ham. His father was once a song-and-dance man for an act called Robertson's Kentucky Minstrels that had once toured the United States. Freddie's father died when he was seven, and the motherless boy grew up in an orphanage. He had already performed in a children's troupe by the time he met Julia.

Julia and Freddie started a ten-year relationship based more on having fun than on commitment. When Julia suggested jokingly that they might as well get married, Freddie surprised her by actually agreeing. The next day he hopped an ocean freighter and was gone for three months. He came home long enough for John to be conceived, then shipped off again. Soon after John's birth, it was obvious that Julia and Freddie's frivolous marriage had ended.

Although they were still officially married, mostly because Freddie was not around long enough for her to divorce him, Julia, an attractive young woman with auburn hair, began frequenting the Liverpool pubs filled with sailors on leave from wartime duty. She had one short-term liaison with a soldier that resulted in a daughter who was given up for adoption, before she met a waiter named John Dykins.

After a showdown with Freddie when in 1945, Julia moved into a tiny flat with her new lover. Mimi, angry that little John had to sleep in a bed with his mother and her lover, reported Julia to Liverpool social service authorities, who ordered that John move to Aunt Mimi's until Julia found a larger apartment.

John was not yet school age but his already topsy-turvy life was upset again a year later when Freddie showed up at the home of Mimi and her husband George Smith. Freddie claimed to be in a repentant mood and Mimi allowed him to take John for what was supposed to be a day-trip to a nearby resort town called Blackpool. But Freddie never returned with John.

After several weeks, Julia tracked him down and confronted Freddie in a heated argument as their five-year-old son watched in tears. Finally, John was asked to make a cruel choice. He was told to decide for himself which parent he wanted to live with. At first, recalling their recent fun on the seashore, and Freddie's promise that they were going to board a ship and sail to New Zealand, John chose his father. A dejected Julia left the Blackpool boardinghouse where Freddy and John were staying. But when the door closed, John, filled with despair at the thought of never seeing his mother again, dashed down the street sobbing, "Mummy, Mummy! Don't go, don't go!" and Julia whisked him back to Liverpool where he was returned to the custody of Aunt Mimi and Uncle George. After painfully having to choose between two parents, John would live with neither.

Lennon grew up in a somewhat upscale neighborhood in Liverpool with his Aunt Mimi and Uncle George.

Unlike Julia, Mimi and George owned a house known as Mendips, in a somewhat upscale neighborhood by Liverpool standards and John had his own room on the second floor. Mimi was as pragmatic as Julia was carefree and ran her household with an iron hand. Uncle George, who ran a local dairy, was a softer touch. "Sometimes when John had done something wrong and I sent him to his room," Mimi recalled, "I'd find George creeping upstairs with the *Beano*, John's favorite comic, and a bar of chocolate."

Mimi loved John deeply and was quick to recognize his intelligence. Both she and Uncle George indulged John's curiosity and thirst for knowledge. It was soon obvious that John was a child to be reckoned with. His first head-master remarked that he was, "sharp as a needle . . . but he won't do anything he doesn't want to." "His mind was going the whole time," added Mimi. "It was always either drawing, or writing poetry, or reading. He was a great reader. It was always books, books, books."

Aunt Mimi and Uncle George taught him to read using the *Liverpool Echo* newspaper, which launched a habit of newspaper reading he kept the rest of his life. As soon as he could read, John began devouring books. Among his favorites was Lewis Carroll's classic *Alice in Wonderland.* He loved the surreal plot and language, and memorized nonsensical passages such as "Jabberwocky," which begins:

Twas brillig, and the slithy toves
Did gyre and gimble in the wabe;
All mimsy were the borogroves,
And the mome raths outgrabe.

John easily became the leader of the other boys in his neighborhood. "He always had to be in charge," Mimi remembered. "Always. The other boys had to be the cow-boys and he *had* to be the Indian. And when he said they were dead, they were dead. 'Pretend properly,' he would tell them."

John's best friend, another precocious boy named Pete Shotton, started out his chief rival. Shotton would taunt John with chants of "Winnie, Winnie!," making fun of John's middle name, which he hated. Soon they were fighting. But after pinning Shotton to the ground, John realized he would make a better friend than enemy. They joined forces and "Shennon and Lotton," as John renamed them, became the scourge of the neighborhood. They convinced the other boys to pool their Sunday pennies that their parents had intended to be placed into the church collection box and buy bubble gum instead. When they got older they climbed a tall tree on Menlove Avenue, John's home street, and swung from a rope in front of approaching double-decker buses. "John, even then, viewed the world almost as a surrealistic carnival," Shotton reports. "Life, to him, was a never-ending stage play, and he would discover something bizarre in even the most mundane event, not to mention the myriad rules and regulations that thwarted our day-to-day pursuit of liberty and happiness."

One of John's favorite places to fantasize was a large Salvation Army orphanage called Strawberry Fields, which he could see from his bedroom window. With Shotton, he clambered over the orphanage's sandstone wall to play in the dense woods and murky, frog-infested pond until they were shooed away by the resident matrons. Inspired by *Huckleberry Finn*, one of Shotton's favorite books, they built a leaky raft to traverse the pond.

Once a summer the Salvation Army held a garden party to raise money for the Strawberry Fields orphanage. His

As a boy, Lennon liked to play in the woods and frog-infested pond at the Salvation Army orphanage, Strawberry Fields, near his house.

aunt recalled, "As soon as we could hear the Salvation Army band starting, John would jump up and down shouting, 'Mimi, come on! We're going to be late!'" He reveled in every aspect of these events, from the thump of the uniformed brass band, to the penny-apiece bottles of lemonade he and his mates were permitted to sell, to the treats they pinched (stole) from the other stands when no one was looking.

John's independent streak, which served him well as gang leader, created trouble at school. He usually did exactly what he wanted, and never felt connected to classroom regimens. He later said, "I used to think, I must be a genius, but nobody's noticed. Either I'm a genius or I'm mad, which is it?"

His report cards had high marks for art and little else. The teacher's comments were not encouraging:

> 1953: "A poor result due to the fact that he spends most of his time devising 'witty' remarks."
> 1955: "He is so fond of obtaining a cheap laugh in class that he has little time left for serious concentration."
> 1956: "He is certainly on the road to failure if this goes on."

His witty remarks, scorned by teachers, were relished by fellow students. John began circulating his own pun-laden underground newspaper, the *Daily Howl*, when he was twelve. Peppered with grotesque, satirical illustrations, and filled with figments of John's imagination, such as Scotsman Fungus MacDungheap, and weather forecasts of, "Yes . . . and no . . . you can't tell, can you? Who cares?" One edition lamented that, "Our late editor is dead; he died of death, which killed him."

By the time John entered Quarry Bank High School for Boys, it was clear that what he excelled at was breaking rules and tormenting teachers. He wore Quarry Bank's school blazer, with its crest that proclaimed in Latin, "From This Rough Metal We Forge Virtue," with irony. Virtue was a word very few people—especially teachers and girls—associated with John Lennon. He later summed up his attitude about the new school: "I looked at all the hundreds of new kids and thought, 'Christ, I'll have to fight my way through all this lot.'"

Fight he did, much to Aunt Mimi's chagrin. One day, as she rode down Penny Lane, the road to the school, she passed a group of scruffs surrounding two boys locked in a fight. Then, she recalls, "they parted and out came this awful boy with his coat hanging off. To my horror, it was John."

Among John's most notorious capers was the hiding of a student in a hollow column of the old school building during a French class. Halfway through the lesson, the victim apparently fainted and fell through the wall. As his transgressions mounted, John was punished with canings, but they soon ended when the school leaders realized he was determined to meet the painful punishment with a smirk, which only raised his prestige among the other boys.

The more perceptive adults, such as Aunt Mimi, realized that John's antics were partly motivated by his need to cover up his feelings. He seldom saw his mother, and his father was long gone. Another problem was his poor eyesight. He hated the round metal-framed granny glasses that were issued to him at no charge by Britain's national health care system. He wore them only when absolutely necessary and usually walked around with a squint that made it look as though he was peering down his rather prominent nose, which aggravated the already disdainful impression he seemed to convey toward much of the world. It also put him at genuine peril. He once ran into the back of a parked vehicle while biking down Menlove Avenue.

John later said that he actually enjoyed seeing the

world through weak eyes. The blurry objects seemed to complement his askew psychological view of the world that he expressed in words and drawings. He even began inducing hazy visions by staring into his bedroom mirror until he fell into a trancelike state.

His trances were often interrupted by Mimi's stern voice. She was determined to shape up her nephew and force him to put his keen intelligence to good work. Conflict was inevitable. There was little middle ground between his aunt's expectations and John's determination to do what he wanted. Mimi felt as strongly as ever that John was capable of great achievement. The question was, in what?

two

Quarry Men

Before long, John developed an ambition, but it wasn't what Aunt Mimi had in mind. He decided that he wanted to be a musician. His interest in music had begun a few years earlier, when one of the college students the Smiths occasionally took in as borders showed John a harmonica. "One of them had a mouth organ," John explained, "and said he'd buy me one if I could learn a tune by the next morning—so I learned about two."

The student purchased John a cheap harmonica. On a holiday bus trip to visit relatives in Scotland, John played it all the way from Liverpool. The driver was so impressed that he presented the boy with a professional quality harmonica someone had left on his bus the week before.

A reunion with his mother strengthened John's love of music. Julia began regularly stopping over at the Smiths' house about the time John entered Quarry Bank when he was twelve. He was surprised to learn that his mother, who he had hardly seen for years, lived only a few minutes down the bus line in a cinder-block public housing project. He had assumed she had moved away from Liverpool.

Lennon reconnected with his mother, Julia, when he was twelve years old. His mother strengthened his newfound love of music. (Courtesy of M Haywood Archives/Redfern)

Any resentment he felt over Julia's neglect was put aside. For the first time in his life, he had a chance to know his mother, who was the opposite of Aunt Mimi. Julia still lived with John Dykins. The couple now had two daughters, and she was as gleefully irresponsible as ever. She didn't have a job, and warned one of her daughters, "Don't ever get a washing machine, lovey. It'll just mean hard, unending work. Always use the Chinese laundry." For John, Julia's attitude was a refreshing change from the strict rules of Aunt Mimi. Mimi was more like a strict mother, while Julia acted like an indulgent young aunt.

When John got a bike, he wheeled over to her house regularly, which became a safe haven when "Shennon and Lotton" were kicked out of school. Afraid to return to their homes after the expulsion, they biked to Julia's and, over cake and Cokes, told her what had happened. "Don't worry about school," she breezily replied. "Don't worry about a thing! Everything's going to work out fine!"

Julia and John shared an offbeat sense of humor. One of her favorite pranks was to wear a pair of spectacles with no glass in the frames. During a conversation with someone on the street, she would nonchalantly rub her eyes through the nonexistent lenses.

John liked Dykins and his two half-sisters as well. Dykins worked as a waiter and would sometimes let John take a lucky dip into a goldfish bowl full of the tips he brought home from the restaurant. Julia and John also shared a love of music. Dykins worked at night, which gave him time to do the domestic chores. This gave Julia plenty of time to sit at her piano and sing. Unlike the classical selections deemed as the only decent music by Aunt Mimi, Julia belted out such songs as "Wedding Bells Are Breaking Up This Old Gang of Mine" and others from minstrel shows, music halls, and movies. She had a phonograph, rare at that time even among wealthier Liverpudlians, and her pride and joy was a mother-of-pearl trimmed banjo that had belonged to her grandfather.

In 1956, when John was fifteen and awakening to popular music, England was gripped by a craze for what became known as skiffle music. Skiffle blended influences ranging from English vaudeville to American folk music. The unifying factor was that it was relatively easy to play. With a guitar at the core, almost any group of inexperienced musicians wielding homemade instruments could soon learn to play skiffle.

John badgered both Mimi and Julia to buy him a guitar, without success. Undaunted, he found a ten dollar model in a catalog and ordered it through the mail. He told both mother and aunt that the other had agreed to the purchase. He defended his investment by pointing out the guitar's inside label that proclaimed, "Guaranteed not to split."

Aunt Mimi was unconvinced. "The guitar's all very well, John," she warned, "but you'll never make a living at it." John was banished to the glass-enclosed front porch, partitioned from the rest of the house, to practice, but soon came to prefer the acoustics and privacy of this space. Mimi swore, "He leaned so long against the brick, I think he must have rubbed part of it off with his backside."

Julia was much more supportive of John's new interest and taught him some chords on the banjo. John even tuned his guitar to the different key of a banjo, and used only five of his instrument's six strings, as his mother had shown him. Before long, he could play a few chords and then a few tunes.

John surmised that almost anyone could bang out skiffle tunes and set out to recruit his friends. Shotton took up the washboard, and another buddy made a bass from a washtub, string and broom. Soon a second guitarist, a banjo player, and a drummer joined them.

The budding musicians decided to call themselves the Quarry Men, in hopes the name would give them an edge to play at Quarry Bank School functions. Lennon was the group's leader, in part because he was the only one bold

*In high school, Lennon (center) and his friend Pete Shotton, along with some other friends, formed the band the Quarry Men. (*Courtesy of the Associated Press)

enough to sing in front of an audience. Their first gig, in 1957, was on the rear end of a truck.

Just as the Quarry Men were learning their first songs, they were blindsided, along with other British teenagers, by a sonic force from America even more powerful than skiffle. It was the pulsating rhythm of rock and roll, delivered with the swivel-hipped authority of Elvis Presley. "Before Elvis there was nothing," John would later proclaim. An exaggeration, perhaps, but Mimi confirmed his state of obsession: "He became a mess almost overnight, and all because of Elvis Presley."

To his aunt's chagrin, John began to mimic Elvis. He greased his hair to set on top of his head in a "D.A." hairdo. (D.A. stood for "duck's ass," because of what it resembled when it was slicked back into a wave that crested upon the wearer's neck.) He also dressed in the "Teddy Boy"

Lennon was highly influenced by rock 'n' roll legend Elvis Presley, who took the world by storm in the late '50s. (Courtesy of the Associated Press)

uniform of skin-tight drainpipe jeans and neon-bright shirts, previously popularized by hoodlums.

In July 1957, the Quarry Men were booked for an afternoon garden party at St. Peter's, Mimi's church. John, fearful Mimi would disapprove of the gig, crept out of the house early.

Mimi, whose husband had died the previous year, attended the event. When she heard a band kick in from across a field, she strolled over and saw her nephew perform for the first time. "I couldn't take my eyes off him," she marveled. "There was this grin all over John's face." She confessed that she was, "pleased as punch to see him up there," and led the applause at the end of the set.

Also in the audience was a fifteen-year-old boy named Paul McCartney, who had been invited by a friend of John's. Paul had a keen interest in the new rock and roll music. He and John met for the first time after the Quarry Men left the stage. Paul had a baby face but had already displayed musical talent. He not only played guitar correctly—in contrast to the banjo chording method John still used—he also knew the words to many of the songs that John had faked his way through that day.

John tried to appear nonchalant as Paul displayed his superior playing skills, ending his demonstration with a screaming Little Richard imitation. But John was not as cool as he had pretended to be. For days, he thought of little else. He knew that Paul could be a huge asset to the Quarry Men, but feared he would threaten his leadership.

John ultimately decided that Paul could not only help the Quarry Men, but could end up hurting them if he joined a rival band. Not wanting to appear too eager, John asked Shotton to invite Paul into the band. Spotting Paul biking past one day, the washboard player said: "By the way, I've been talking to John about it and . . . we thought maybe you'd like to join the group." A full minute passed as Paul pretended to be weighing the decision. "Oh, all right," he shrugged, and cycled home.

On the surface, John and Paul had little in common, other than their love of music and their D.A. hairdos. Paul was more conscientious in his studies, and obedient to his elders. (He wasn't allowed to officially join the band until he returned from scout camp, two months later.) Paul's father had warned him to, "Be careful of that John Lennon. He could get you into trouble." However, the two boys soon discovered that their musical connection was stronger than these differences.

Paul helped to lift the Quarry Men's sound to a new level. They rehearsed whenever and wherever they could, frequently in the tiny bathroom of Julia's house because the wall tiles and linoleum floor provided sound insulation. John's half sister remembers the enterprising lads looking, "like a comedy act. They would be squeezed into the bath, perched up on top of the loo seat, propped up against the hand basin, squatted on the floor, and standing with one leg up on the edge of the bath to support a guitar."

Looking to improve the Quarry Men, Paul introduced the band to a young guitarist named George Harrison.

Only fourteen, George could actually play melodies, not just the accompanying chords, on his guitar. George quickly came to regard John with unabashed awe and John, for his part, was glad that there wasn't the same rivalry between them that existed between him and Paul.

The only problem was George's age. Now seventeen, John worried about how it would look to have such a little kid in his band. He stalled his decision for weeks, but George continued to hang around. When George was finally invited to John's house, his hot pink shirt and winklepicker (pointy-toed) shoes instantly triggered disapproval from Aunt Mimi. This sealed the deal—George was in.

As the Quarry Men's lineup changed to include more skilled players, the founding members lost their places. Shotton was ready to go. He had only joined to please his best friend. Though John agreed to his leaving, Shotton's departure was awkward because neither of the boys—who once tried to be blood brothers—had ever quit anything they'd started together. The matter was finally settled when the Quarry Men played a party that offered free beer. After guzzling three or four glasses each John broke the washboard over Shotton's head. "Well, that takes care of that problem, doesn't it, Pete?" he said, as Shotton laughed.

"I knew," Shotton said later, "that the destruction of my washboard, which I certainly wasn't about to repair or replace, had effectively released me from all further obligations as a Quarry Man."

John's obsession with music replaced what little attention he had paid to high school. He failed a series of exams designed to place British students in college. His only option was art school, which sometimes waived academic requirements for talented students. Mimi hoped art school might push John towards a more promising career than rock and roll. John, however, evaluated the opportunity as his mother might have—it seemed too much like work.

Then one day when he ran into a former classmate, who was now in his first year at the Liverpool College of Art. "You should try to get into art school," raved his friend. "I'm having a marvelous time drawing nudes." John soon enrolled.

Nevertheless, John regarded art school as little more than a diversion. His primary focus was music. His talent was developing rapidly, in no small part due to his musical partnership with Paul. Pete Shotton observed later that, "Though I have yet to encounter a personality as strong and individualistic as John's, he always had to have a partner. He never could abide the thought of getting stuck out on his limb all by himself."

This was a happy time for John. He lived a carefree life, surrounded by close friends. His family life was also as good as it had ever been. His mother and his aunt were closer than ever, and both were proud to see the young man they had raised in art school, happy, and seemingly destined for a good life.

It was not to last. One night, in July 1958, Julia spent the evening at Mimi's while John waited back at his mother's house with his half sisters. As usual, the conversation between Julia and Mimi focused on John. Mimi still worried about John. "Don't worry," Julia assured her as she left.

Then, as Julia crossed Menlove Avenue, she was struck and killed by a car. It was being driven by a police officer who was driving without a license; he saw Julia in the road, and accidentally pressed on the accelerator instead of the brake.

A policeman showed up at her house a little later to inform John and his stepsisters that their forty-four-year-old mother was dead. John was devastated.

"I lost her twice," he later explained. "Once as a five-year-old when I was moved in with my auntie. And once again at seventeen when she actually, physically died. It just absolutely made me *very*, very bitter. The underlying chip on my shoulder that I had as a youth got *really* big then."

three
Birth of
the Beatles

Julia's death, coming so soon after he had finally established a relationship with her, was devastating to John. But he put on a brave face. He sought, and received, no sympathy and only cursory condolences from most people and, because of his often-abrasive personality, most people were afraid to say anything to him.

One person did grow closer to him after Julia's death. Paul McCartney had lost his own mother to cancer only a few years earlier and was able to understand what his new friend was suffering. "There was a famous expression, 'Don't *real* on me, man," McCartney explained later. "He loved his mum more than anything, but at that age, you're not allowed to be devastated, particularly not teenage boys. You just shrug it off. I know he had private tears. We were like wounded animals, and just by looking at each other, we knew the pain that the other was feeling, but we weren't going to break down and cry because you just didn't do that kind of thing."

Lennon began to seek solace in alcohol. Now of the legal drinking age, and out of Aunt Mimi's control, he spent many of his days getting drunk at art college hangouts. Alcohol unleashed Lennon's pent-up anger, which often revealed itself in abusive insults. He took to mocking the gaits of crippled people to their faces, and one drunken night told a Jewish piano player, "They should've stuck you in the ovens with the rest of 'em!" a reference to Hitler's murder of Jews. These cruel remarks masked Lennon's own fear that he was a freak, outside the mainstream, who had never known peace or contentment.

Pete Shotton, who was attending the police academy and seeing his old friend less frequently, was alarmed at John's growing dependence on alcohol. One night he hopped on a bus and found Lennon passed out on the back seat. After carrying his old friend home, Shotton had to admit, "Even I sometimes worried that he seemed destined for Skid Row."

Lennon was able to find some peace in music. He spent many hours strumming his guitar in an open plaza, often in the company of McCartney and Harrison. Listeners were enthralled by the latest rock and roll numbers he strummed, many of which he memorized from broadcasts of Radio Luxembourg, a faraway underground radio station. Many students in Liverpool first heard the music of American rock and rollers such as Chuck Berry, Buddy Holly, and Ray Charles through the voice of John Lennon.

Lennon's rebellious image and sarcastic jabs turned off plenty of people, but some girls found his bad boy image attractive. One who did was an auburn-haired girl named Cynthia Powell, a student at the art school who lived "over the water," as Liverpudlians described the more affluent suburb of Hoylake located across the Mersey River. Cynthia was polite, neatly dressed, mild mannered—everything Lennon wasn't. Her first impression when she saw him was, "that I had nothing in common with this individual. He frightened me to death."

Lennon categorized Cynthia as, "a right Hoylake runt, dead snobby. We used to poke fun at her and mock her." In truth, she reminded him of the French actress Brigitte Bardot, his ideal woman. During Lennon's second year of college they shared a class, but several months passed before he asked her to go with him to a school dance. On their first date Lennon invited her to a party the next day, but Cynthia panicked and lied that she was engaged.

"I didn't ask you to marry me," Lennon responded and Cynthia relented. They soon began a serious relationship—albeit one that did not always go smoothly. Lennon had a volatile temper and liked to flirt with other girls. At the same time he became jealous if he suspected her of chatting up another man. "I was in sort of a blind rage for two years," Lennon admitted. "I was either drunk or fighting. It was the same with other girlfriends I had. There was something the matter with me."

Cynthia broke up with him once, but soon they were back together. She even dyed her hair blond to match

Brigitte Bardot's. Both still lived at home, so they often sought privacy at the crash pad of Lennon's art school friend, Stuart Sutcliffe. Sutcliffe had a slight physique that was accentuated by his skin-tight jeans and pink shirts. He wore sunglasses day and night, and was considered one of the best artists in the school.

Lennon and Sutcliffe became close friends. Lennon considered Sutcliffe to be the superior artist and respected him more than he did the school's instructors. Sutcliffe, on the other hand, loved rock music but did not have John's musical talent.

When Lennon was nineteen, he moved into Sutcliffe's flat, which was sort of a commune for any art student needing housing. Among the coal-burning fireplace, life-sized canvasses, and dingy mattresses was a satin-lined coffin where Lennon often slept. A local tabloid even ran an article entitled "The Beatnik Horror" that was accompanied by a photo of the squalid room. Lying in the center was a beatnik whom Lennon happily recognized as himself.

Though Lennon continued his pursuit of art largely through Sutliffe's encouragement, he was more interested in rock and roll. McCartney, who was about to finish high school, was equally committed to music, and young George Harrison was ready to drop out of school before graduating if the Quarry Men could find enough work to play full time.

The group memorized the latest hits from American rockers. They also began to write songs of their own. Paul, who was the more organized, would carefully jot down words and music into an exercise book. Then he and John would work on the songs together. Because of the collaborative method they used, they had a handshake agreement that everything they wrote together, regardless of who made the most individual contributions to each song, would have the same songwriting credit of Lennon/McCartney.

"We wrote a *lot* of stuff together, one-on-one, eyeball-to-eyeball," Lennon said. The duo wrote about one hundred songs in a year, most of which were lost when McCartney's girlfriend accidentally threw them in the garbage.

Cynthia later looked back on Lennon and McCartney's formative years as "a beautiful period. . . . Their harmonies were so beautiful. John had this image of being the toughest guy in college but his music showed what all of us knew underneath. He had a gentleness that needed to come out, and it did in those songs."

To the chagrin of the few instructors who supported him, Lennon increasingly ignored his schoolwork and his artistic talents were not developed. Many on the faculty were angry that John distracted Stuart Sutcliffe, the school's star pupil. Suttcliffe often skipped school to hang out at band practices and slept in mornings after their late night gigs.

The band decided that the Quarry Men name needed to go. It reminded them of their high school roots. They tried out several new names, such as Johnny and the Moondogs, but nothing stuck. Then Sutcliffe suggested The Beetles, a homage to The Crickets, the backup band of Buddy Holly, one of their favorite American rockers. The final twist of

Buddy Holly and the Crickets were one of Lennon's favorite bands. "The Beatles" is a nod to the Crickets. (Courtesy of Pictorial Press)

their name came when Lennon, with his typical fondness for puns, changed the spelling to the Beatles, as a way to connect with the beat groups, as rock 'n' roll bands in Liverpool were being called.

Lennon wanted to shift the band away from skiffle music, which had lost its popularity among young Brits. He got rid of the washtub bass, hoping to replace it with an electric instrument like the amplified guitars he, McCartney, and Harrison now played. But they did not have enough money to buy a new instrument. Sutcliffe came to their rescue. He used the $120 he had been paid for one of his paintings—an astronomical sum for a student work in those days—and bought an electric bass. This was effectively the end of his art school education.

Stuart Sutcliffe (front) *with Harrison* (left) *and Lennon in Hamburg, Germany* (Courtesy of K&K Ulf Kruger Ohg/Redferns)

Much like Pete Shotton had been a few years before, Sutcliffe was recruited on the basis of friendship, not musical talent. Though he was willing to learn, he was not a quick study. During gigs he hid behind sunglasses and turned away from the audience to hide his fumbling fingers. But he had the proper look, and the Beatles became regular—if not well-paid—performers at Liverpool clubs and dance halls. "We were making about ten bob (about $1.50) a night, plus as much eggs on toast and Coke as we could take," Harrison later remembered.

In May 1960, the Beatles got their first chance to play out of town. It wasn't much of an opportunity, only a two-week stint backing a minor British pop singer at a series of shows in northern Scotland. The tour was especially hard on the Beatles' newly recruited drummer, Tommy Moore. The van transporting the band through the Scottish Highlands crashed and he ended up in the hospital with facial cuts and missing teeth. When they returned to Liverpool, Moore's wife made him quit the band for a real job on the night shift at a local bottling plant.

Her demand was not unreasonable. The Beatles played rowdy venues, such as the Grosvenor Ballroom, a dive so rough that chairs were fastened together in groups of four so they couldn't be thrown during fights. One night, Sutcliffe was knocked down and kicked in the head by a gang for attracting the attention of one of their birds, slang for girlfriends. Lennon flew into a rage, and pummeled the assailants until his bandmates were able to pull him away.

Despite the less than glamorous venues, their work was beginning to pay off. Within a few months, they got another invitation to hit the road, this time to Hamburg, Germany. Hamburg was a big, bustling seaport, full of sailors and other transients, and it had one of the most uproarious entertainment districts in all of Europe. Hamburg clubs owners needed good rock and roll bands and were willing to import beat groups from all over Europe to provide it.

When the Hamburg opportunity came the Beatles were still short a drummer, as they often were. "We had all sorts of drummers at the time," Lennon explained, "because

Pete Best, an early drummer for the Beatles
(Courtesy of M Haywood Archives/Redferns)

drum kits were few and far between. It was an expensive item. They were usually idiots." Even Paul tried drumming for a time. Spurred by the Hamburg invitation, the Beatles nicked Pete Best from a band that played mostly at Best's mother's coffee bar, the Casbah. The Beatles, whose ages ranged from seventeen to nineteen, were on their way to Hamburg, Germany.

The Hamburg promoter, Bruno Koschmider, a former circus clown, had promised them free housing, which turned out to be a tiny space behind the screen at his Bambi Cinema, a run-down movie house. "You could just about swing a cat in there," joked Paul, "providing it's got no tail." They had to use the same shabby bathrooms as the customers. "We'd try to get into the ladies' first, which was cleanest, but fat old German women would push past us."

Lennon remembered that after a late night of work, the tenant musicians were often awakened by the sounds of a western movie blaring on the screen outside.

This poster for the Kaiserkeller club in Hamburg, Germany, lists the Beatles and several other bands that played in the rowdy club.

They were booked to play at the Indra, a former strip joint and possibly the quietest club in Hamburg's red-light district, the Reeperbahn. The Indra's management hoped a young rock band might bring more business. Their first night left the half-dozen patrons less than impressed, and the agitated promoter exhorted the band to "Mach schau!"—"make a show"—to attract customers.

Lennon began jumping all over the tiny stage, and soon the other Beatles joined him. Lennon answered the crowd's applause with stiff-armed shouts of "Heil Hitler!"—a reminder of the Nazi Germany of a generation ago—and they seemed to love it. He once returned to stage from the bathroom with a toilet seat around his neck. They cranked their amps to full blast, which occasionally triggered a shower of sparks from Harrison's unit. Because the Beatles' grueling contract called for six forty-five minute sets each evening, they stretched three-minute rock and roll numbers into twenty-minute epics. Word got around about the hot group the Germans called "Da Peedles," and the Indra was soon packed. When the neighbors began to complain that the place was too noisy, even for the raucous Reeperbahn, the Beatles were booked into a larger club down the street and the strippers, seen as more sedate entertainment, returned to the Indra.

The Kaiserkeller, bigger, louder, and rowdier than the Indra, was run by a German ex-boxing champion who hired many of his sparring partners as waiters. Fights broke out almost nightly, and the patrons and the staff spilled blood.

Richard Starkey, aka, Ringo Starr, (second from left) first met the members of the Beatles while drumming with Rory Storm and the Hurricanes in Hamburg, Germany. (Courtesy of Pictorial Press)

At the Kaiserkeller, the Beatles alternated their six sets with those of another Liverpool band, Rory Storm and the Hurricanes. Because there was no time to go anywhere in the sixty minutes between their sets, the bandmates spent twelve-hour days at the club.

Lennon befriended the other band, and particularly liked their affable drummer, Richard Starkey, who performed under the name "Ringo" Starr, a nickname he got because he wore rings on every finger. The flamboyant drummer also sported a beard and a silver streak in his hair. Underneath the glitz, though, Starr was easygoing and friendly. In contrast to the Beatles' own often-sullen drummer Pete Best, Starr seemed to "roll with it."

To help get through the long days, John and the other members began taking German diet pills known as "Prellies." These fat-reducing stimulants kept people awake when taken in large doses. Lennon and his mates washed the pills down with the free beer they received at the Kaiserkeller, and whatever food they could scrounge from the waiters.

Lennon told about the band's hard living in almost-daily love letters back home to Cynthia. He also expressed his longing and loneliness though silly rhymes such as, "Postman, postman, don't be slow; I'm in love with Cyn, so go, man go!" He might have been in love with the girl back home, but that didn't stop Lennon and his bandmates from taking advantage of the female companionship readily available in the Reeperbahn.

Stuart Sutcliffe, however, had a steady German girl-friend. Astrid Kirchherr was a young photography student who had wandered into the Kaiserkeller by chance one night and became a fan of the Beatles. Sutcliffe soon fell in love with her, and began spending much of his time in her company.

Astrid styled his hair in a French fashion that was combed forward, instead of piled on top of the head in a D.A. Soon Lennon and the others—except Best—wore their hair in these shaggy mop tops.

Sutcliffe asked Kirchherr to marry him and moved into a spare room in her mother's house. No longer living with his bandmates, and still failing to make much progress as a musician, Sutcliffe was growing apart from the group.

McCartney was particularly critical of Sutcliffe, and felt he was holding back the band.

Lennon was caught in the middle. He understood and agreed with McCartney's concern for the band's development, but he was attached to Sutcliffe, who had been his best friend for some time. He feared that kicking Sutcliffe out of the band might cause him to lose another close companion. Tensions soon erupted into an onstage fight. Lennon realized that something had to be done but, as had happened so many times in his life, fate intervened at a critical juncture, this time in the form of German authorities.

When the Beatles sat in with the band of a Liverpool musician and friend, Tony Sheridan, at the Top Ten Club, one of the Kaiserkeller's top competitors, their promoter, Koschmider, was enraged. He saw to it that seventeen-year-old Harrison was deported for working underage in Germany as a foreigner, though George's age had been well-known for months. Koschmider then elevated a small accident at the Bambi into an arson charge against McCartney and Best, and they fled to Liverpool. Without his band, Lennon had little choice but to head back to Liverpool himself.

Sutcliffe, however, was not willing to leave his fiancé, and decided to stay in Hamburg, even if that meant leaving the band. Lennon bid him farewell, and headed home.

John spent his remaining money on train fare to Liverpool. After regaling his Aunt Mimi with glowing accounts of the Beatles' success in Hamburg in letters, Lennon had to ask her for money to pay the cabbie that brought him home from the train station.

Lennon spent his first week back in Liverpool enjoying Mimi's cooking and Cynthia's company, and sleeping. Before long, though, his focus was back on music.

"Once his mind was set on something," Mimi noted, "nobody and nothing could shake him. He was down but not out."

Lennon was pleased to learn that news had spread across Liverpool about their popularity in the German clubs. The band's sound had improved when McCartney switched to bass guitar and the newly focused Beatles were now in the top rank of Liverpool bands. They started playing bigger and better local venues, such as the Cavern Club, a onetime produce warehouse that had been converted into a club. For young Liverpudlians in 1961, it was the place to be.

"It was great," attests Gerry Marsden, who used to play the Cavern as leader of Gerry and the Pacemakers. "It was a small, smelly cellar that looked like a train tunnel, basically. All the kids came down and it stank of disinfectant because they used to clean it out with tons of the stuff." The heat generated by sweaty bodies packed elbow to elbow condensed on the brick ceiling and walls of the windowless room, then fell as "Cavern rain."

The Beatles were the featured act at a noontime show that was often packed with teens and young adults on lunch breaks. Their sound honed by hundreds of performances in Hamburg, they were an older, wiser and more talented band. It also helped that they were now able to compress their energy into an hour's performance, instead of having to stretch it out across six daily sets. As Lennon observed years later, "I was raised in Liverpool, but I grew up in Hamburg."

The Beatles soon had a chance to return to Hamburg, this time as headliners at the Top Ten Club. As they bounced back and forth between the two cities they began gaining notoriety in both.

Lennon was still discontented, however. In a letter to Sutcliffe, he wrote:

> "I can't remember anything without a sadness so deep
> That it hardly becomes known to me.
> So deep that its tears leave me a spectator
> Of my own stupidity.
> And so I go rambling on
> With a hey nonny nonno no."

Despite Lennon's inner sadness, which he usually kept hidden from those around him, his life was about to change. One day in October 1961, a Cavern fan walked into the nearby Northern England Music Shop (NEMS) and asked to buy a 45 rpm record called "My Bonnie" by the Beatles. The manager, Brian Epstein, had no idea what the customer was talking about. Epstein had always prided himself on being able to obtain any record a customer requested. He scribbled a note: "My Bonnie. The Beatles. Check on Monday." After some searching, Epstein learned that the record was actually a single cut in Hamburg by Tony Sheridan, with his friends the Beatles providing backup. He stocked the record, and it outsold even the latest releases by Elvis Presley.

Epstein was surprised when a buyer told him that these same Beatles played almost everyday only a block away at the Cavern Club. Twenty-seven-year-old Epstein's tastes leaned toward classical music, but the businessman in him was compelled to check out this hot-selling band.

At the Cavern, Epstein recognized the Beatles immediately as the scruffs who hung out in his store and never bought anything. "I had been bothered a little," he said, "by the frequent visits of a group of scruffy lads in leather and jeans . . . chatting to the girls and lounging on the counters listening to records. They were pleasant enough boys, untidy and a little wild, and they needed haircuts."

Epstein's impression of the Beatles didn't change right away. "They smoked as they played, and they ate and talked and pretended to hit each other. They turned their backs and shouted at people, and laughed at their private jokes. But there was quite clearly enormous excitement. They seemed to give off some sort of personal magnetism. I was fascinated by them." He especially noted how Lennon seemed to control an audience at will, even as he hurled insults at them.

Epstein returned to the Cavern several times over the next month. He began to toy with the idea of managing the Beatles. Epstein knew little about rock and roll and less about handling a band, but he was bored with running his family-owned record store and relished the challenge of getting in on the ground floor of something potentially big.

Epstein invited the four band members to his office for a chat. A half hour after the appointed time, there was still

Brian Epstein became the Beatles' manager after hearing them play at the Cavern Club several times. (Courtesy of John Rodgers/Redferns)

no sign of McCartney. Harrison gave him a call, and relayed the fact that he was in the bath. "This is disgraceful," huffed the punctual Epstein. "He's going to be very late."

"Late," Harrison agreed, "but very clean."

When McCartney finally showed up they discussed the future of the Beatles. It took a week before Epstein formally offered his services at another meeting. They all hesitated, and looked to Lennon to make the decision. Finally he announced, "Right, then, Brian, manage us now." Neither the four musicians nor Epstein quite knew what that meant.

four
Beatlemania

As the Beatles' new manager, Brian Epstein began working on moving them beyond Liverpool and Hamburg. But first he decided they had to literally clean up their act. Epstein laid down some new rules: no eating or drinking on stage, no chattering back and forth to each other, and no pelting the audience with verbal abuse. Crowds of regulars tolerated such behavior, but Epstein feared it would turn off potential new fans. He wanted their sets to be more tight and professional.

Epstein, a former drama student, also directed the band to join together, arm in arm, and take a big bow at the end of every set.

Lennon agreed to these changes, but balked at Epstein's final suggestion. He told the band they had to abandon their customary leather jackets and pants, and to be fitted instead with mohair suits. McCartney was accepting of the change. "I'll wear a bloody balloon if someone's going to pay me," he remarked. "I'm not in love with leather *that* much."

When Brian Epstein became the manager for the Beatles, he convinced them to wear suits to enhance their stage persona. (Courtesy of K&K Ulf Kruger Ohg/Redferns)

Lennon was hard to convince, though. "I'd say to George, 'Look, we don't need these suits. Let's chuck them out the window.' My little rebellion was to have my tie loose with the top button of my shirt undone, but Paul'd always come up to me and put it straight." Lennon eventually relented. The cooperation was rewarded when Epstein got the Beatles' fee at the Cavern increased to almost three times their previous pay.

In addition to finding them better gigs, Epstein's other goal, which everyone cheered, was to land them a recording contract. This was not an easy task. The problem was not in getting the ear of British recording companies, especially since Epstein's family owned seven NEMS record stores that ordered their merchandise. The challenge was in convincing record company executives that the Beatles were a worthwhile rock and roll band.

On New Year's Day, 1962, the four nervous Beatles spent twelve hours auditioning at Decca Records. Wanting to play it safe, Epstein chose older, more conservative songs for the band to play. The resulting fifteen-song demo tape contained only two Lennon/McCartney compositions, and little that could be called rock and roll.

Decca was the first company to turn down the Beatles, which infuriated Epstein. "He told me they didn't like the sound," fumed the Beatles' manager. "Groups of guitars were on the way out. I told him I was completely confident that these boys were going to be bigger than Elvis Presley." Lennon laid the blame for the failure on Epstein, who he said had chosen tired material that reflected none of the Beatles' energy.

The Beatles were facing tremendous competition. About four hundred beat groups were operating in and around Liverpool, one for every thousand people. The same was true for cities all over England. With so many groups vying for attention, the Beatles were spurned by almost every record company in the United Kingdom.

They refused to give up and between gigs in Liverpool and Hamburg continued trying to get a contract. Eventually, they came to Parlophone, a small division of British recording giant EMI. Parlophone was best known for records by comedians such as Peter Sellers, the star of Lennon's favorite TV program, *The Goon Show*. At Parlophone, the Beatles auditioned for George Martin, a classically trained producer. Martin saw potential. "I thought they were great," Martin acknowledged. "Not because of their music, because their music wasn't great. But they had this enormous charisma. It felt good to be with them, and I said to myself, 'If I feel like that, the audience is going to feel like that.'"

After lecturing them on the need to upgrade their equipment and to conform to professional recording standards, he asked if they had any concerns about him. They looked at each other, and then Harrison said, "Yeah, I don't like your tie!"

After the audition the Beatles returned to Hamburg where Epstein soon telegraphed them the good news. They had been signed to a recording contract with Parlophone. Three sent back excited postcards:

> McCartney: "Please wire 10,000 pounds (about $18,000) advance royalties."
> Harrison: "Please order four new guitars."
> Lennon: "When are we going to be millionaires?"

Things were picking up for the Beatles. In Hamburg they were booked to play the new Star Club on bills with Little Richard, one of their heroes. Epstein had even paid to have them flown from Liverpool to Hamburg, instead of making them take the cheaper train.

Lennon married Cynthia Powell, his girlfriend of six years, in 1962. (Courtesy of Cummings Archives/Redferns)

When they arrived at the airport, Stuart Sutcliffe's fiancé was waiting with tragic news. Their former bandmate, and John's best friend, had died suddenly of a brain hemorrhage only days earlier. Unable to maintain a stoic face, Lennon wept like a child.

A few months later, Lennon found out that Cynthia was pregnant. He'd been with Cynthia for years, but he was not prepared for marriage and fatherhood. "I don't think we'd have married if I hadn't become pregnant," Cynthia later admitted. "He wasn't the sort at the age of twenty-one to say: 'Will you marry me?' It was all so immediate we hardly realized the seriousness of it all: making love, getting pregnant, getting married."

"Oh Christ, I don't really want to get married, Mimi," he moaned in to his aunt the night before his August 23 wedding.

"Maybe so," she replied, "but what's done is done."

Cynthia later remembered the day as, "more like a funeral than a wedding." Lennon, McCartney and Harrison fidgeted nervously in their matching black suits and ties and a workman outside turned on a jackhammer precisely as the bride and groom exchanged vows.

"None of us heard a word of the service," Cynthia lamented. "We couldn't even hear ourselves think. Trying to keep straight faces and our minds on the enormity of the step we were taking was an impossibility. All we wanted to do was get out and have it over with as soon as possible. It was all totally unreal."

Lennon was distracted from his new marriage and impending fatherhood by the Beatles recording contract. Some two weeks after the wedding, he, McCartney, and Harrison traveled down to EMI's Abbey Road studio in London. The band had recently undergone another change. Drummer Pete Best had been fired. The official word was that George Martin had not liked his drumming, but the entire band had long been unhappy with Best. They preferred Ringo Starr, whose laid-back personality was more compatible with theirs. Fortunately, Starr was between bands and accepted their invitation to become a Beatle. The three original members left it up to Epstein to tell Best that he was out. "We were cowards when we sacked him," Lennon admitted. "But if we had told Pete to his face, that would have been much nastier than getting Brian to do it. It probably would have ended in a fight."

For their first single they chose a Lennon/McCartney composition written back in 1958 called "Love Me Do." The song featured a harmonica riff, unusual for a beat record, played by Lennon, and the three-part harmony vocals that would become integral to the band's sound.

"Love Me Do" was released in October 1962 and inched its way to number seventeen on the British music charts. The Beatles were overjoyed. Harrison woke his parents at two in the morning, hollering that Radio Luxembourg had just played their song. Upon seeing the song listed on the top twenty charts, Lennon said, "They're buying our record. Real people are buying our record!"

Martin hauled them back to the studio in November to record a follow up. This time they clashed with Martin over the choice of the next single. Martin favored a song called, "How Do You Do It," written by a professional songwriter. The band wanted to record another Lennon/McCartney song.

"I told them that they were turning down a hit," Martin recalled. "It was their funeral, but if they were going to be so obstinate then they had better produce something better themselves." The band suggested "Please Please Me," a fast and energetic song they knew their fans liked. After hearing it played, Martin was convinced the boys had been right and said, "Gentlemen, you've made your first number one record!"

Martin's prediction proved to be correct. "Please Please Me" made it to number one on most British charts, while "How Do You Do It?" was eventually recorded by another Liverpool band, Gerry & the Pacemakers, and did the same. Martin had to admit, though, that it was much more important that the Beatles had produced a hit that reflected their own sound and bolstered their reputations as songwriters.

As "Please Please Me" scaled the charts early in 1963, the Beatles were getting ready to hit the road with their biggest tour yet, opening for sixteen-year-old star Helen Shapiro. A novelty singer who attracted attention because of her big voice and young age, Shapiro already had two, number one British songs to her credit.

Though they were supposed to warm up the crowd for Shapiro, the Beatles ended up stealing the show. Portraying themselves as lovable amateurs, with high energy and amiable grins, the quartet of attractive, well-dressed young men were an immediate hit. The crowds went crazy. They made a particularly strong impression on women. In Scotland, girls began screaming at them—with staggering enthusiasm—for no apparent reason. "I suppose they haven't got much else to do up there," Lennon said. The Beatles were amazed, though, that they could inspire this type of frenzy in audiences who had never seen them.

Having played together almost daily for five years, the Beatles knew exactly how to maximize their effect on stage. Typically, they ended their set with a cover of the American rhythm and blues song "Twist and Shout." As

Lennon screamed through the song, girls stormed the stage. Newspapers reported riots, only increasing the frenzy and anticipation at the next show.

Helen Shapiro didn't mind being upstaged by her warm-up act. Being the same age as many of the girls in the audience, she was infatuated by the Beatles herself, especially Lennon, whom she found to be unlike the tough

Lennon spends time backstage with Helen Shapiro. (Courtesy of David Redfern/Redferns)

guy image he liked to project. Instead of gloating over the Beatles triumph during what was supposed to have been her tour, he acted like a protective big brother. Once, when she opened a major British music magazine to a headline that asked, "Is Helen a Has-Been at Sixteen?" he comforted her with, "Don't let the swines get you down."

"He's not the brute and the bully that some folk take him to be," she insisted. "Someday he'll make a great dad and a marvelous husband for some woman."

Like almost everyone else, Shapiro did not know that Lennon was already married, and about to become a father. Epstein had asked Lennon to keep his marriage a secret because he thought a pregnant wife would turn off female fans. Lennon was willing to comply with this request. He later confessed, "Walking about married was like walking about with odd socks on or your fly open."

Cynthia, meanwhile, moved to Aunt Mimi's during her lonely pregnancy. Lennon was on tour when his son was born, and didn't see him for three days. Upon returning, he insisted on naming him Julian after his departed mother, Julia, and fawned over him, saying, "Who's going to be a famous little rocker like his dad?" Then, after a short rest, the new father returned to the road.

The Beatles returned to Abbey Road studios to record an album. The record company, skeptical of the Beatles long term appeal, would only pay to keep the band in the studio for a short time, and Martin didn't press for more. He wanted to capture the energy of a live Beatles performance.

In one nonstop, twelve-hour studio session, the Beatles recorded the songs for their debut album, entitled *Please Please Me*. The album included the singles "Love Me Do" and "Please Please Me," as well as live favorites like "I Saw Her Standing There" and "Twist and Shout."

Released in May 1963, *Please Please Me* shot to the top of the British charts, where it remained for thirty weeks. No recording artist, even American legends such as Elvis, had so dominated the British music scene. The

Beatles were suddenly the most famous young people in England.

In May, they toured with one of their American heroes, Roy Orbison, and, almost to their embarrassment, topped the bill. The press, who labeled the phenomenon "Beatlemania," covered everything they did or said. Harrison made the mistake of divulging a fondness for jellybeans. Soon frenzied girls flung them at the stage during each concert.

The Beatles were recruited to play at London's Royal Variety Performance, an annual benefit hosted by Queen Elizabeth II. The Beatles, who were by now being called the "Fab Four" by newspapers, were the youngest act in an evening of aging performers. Young Beatlemaniacs or their parents snapped up so many of the seats that, for the first time, screams erupted during this normally restrained evening. Lennon announced, "Will the people in the cheaper seats clap your hands?" Then he looked up toward the Royal Box and said: "All the rest of you, if you'll just rattle your jewelry."

Epstein worried that Lennon's light mockery of the Royal Family would lead to backlash, but everyone, from the Royal Family themselves to the twenty-six million people watching the event on television, thought Lennon's behavior was refreshing. The band was suddenly seen not only as a fun rock group, but also as intelligent young men. As a result, their already immense popularity increased even more.

The London *Daily Mirror* said: "*Yeah! Yeah! Yeah!* You have to be a real square not to love the nutty, noisy, happy, handsome Beatles. If they don't sweep your blues away brother, you're a lost cause. If they don't put a beat in your feet sister, you're not living."

Please Please Me stayed number one on the pop charts until it knocked down by its follow-up, *With the Beatles*, which stayed at number one for twenty-one weeks. Epstein and the Beatles had achieved an unthinkable level of success in little over a year. Their popularity spread, and by the end of 1962 the Beatles were the biggest band in Europe.

It was time to conquer America. This was a daunting challenge. In 1962 rock 'n' roll was pure American, a mixture of the blues, jazz, country and western, and gospel music created by African Americans and poor whites in the American South. Ever since it exploded on the scene in the mid-1950s, the United States had produced the biggest rock stars. Not surprisingly, most American fans were skeptical that Brits could rock. The single "Please Please Me," which soared to number one in England, didn't even crack the Top 40 when released in the U.S. in February 1963.

Epstein was determined, however, and traveled to America to build up interest in the Beatles. On the trip he managed to talk a major U.S. record company, Capitol, into releasing the Beatles upcoming single, "I Want to Hold Your Hand."

Epstein also struck an important deal with Ed Sullivan, whose *Ed Sullivan Show* was one of the most popular on American television. Sullivan had been the first to expose Elvis to a huge nationwide audience in 1956. Sullivan

The Beatles performed on The Ed Sullivan Show *in February, 1964.* (Courtesy of the Associated Press)

had been in Sweden during the Beatles' recent tour and noted the stir they created. He agreed to book them for two television appearances beginning February 9, 1964. Epstein insisted on top billing for the Beatles, and accepted a third of Sullivan's usual performer fee in return for the privilege.

Capitol released, "I Want to Hold Your Hand" the day after Christmas, 1963. Because the band was coming to the U.S. for the first time to play not just the *Ed Sullivan Show* but also other venues Epstein had lined up, including New York's Carnegie Hall, the company plastered five million posters that proclaimed, "The Beatles Are Coming!" all over the U.S. They also issued full sets of Beatles singles to hundreds of radio stations. American teens, spurred by this aggressive advertising and footage of British teens going crazy for the band, were dying to find out more about the Beatles.

On February 7, 1964, the Beatles flew to New York. Lennon was accompanied for the first time on tour by Cynthia, who was finally allowed to come out of marital hiding after the London press had discovered that the Beatles' leader was a husband and father.

When the four musicians emerged from their plane in New York they were greeted by a crowd that shrieked so loud they thought for a moment that the jet engines were still on. But the sound was coming from more than

The Beatles arrived to thousands of screaming fans in New York in 1964. This was their first visit to the U.S. (Courtesy of the Associated Press)

ten thousand girls screaming at the top of their lungs while New York police struggled to hold them back.

The Beatles were taken to a pressroom, where they cheekily answered reporters' questions. *"What do you think of Beethoven?"* "Great," they answered, "especially his poems."

"In Detroit, there's people handing out car stickers saying, 'Stamp Out the Beatles.'" "Yeah, well we're bringing out a 'Stamp Out Detroit' campaign."

"Are you going to get a haircut at all?" "I had one yesterday."

"Which do you consider the greatest danger to your careers, nuclear bombs or dandruff?" "Bombs. We've already got dandruff."

The rest of America got their first look at the Beatles two days later. *The Ed Sullivan Show* had received more than fifty thousand requests for the 728 seats available for its Sunday, February 9 program. Sullivan, thrilled that his gamble on the band had paid off so hugely, gave the Beatles an unusually large space to perform five songs in two different time spots on his show. Their names had to be keyed over the television screen as they played—Lennon's i.d. included, "Sorry girls, he's married."

More than 73 million viewers—the largest television audience in history—had tuned in to see the Beatles. It was even reported that no serious crime was committed by a minor anywhere in the U.S. during the hour of *The Ed Sullivan Show.* Monday morning, the Beatles were the talk of nearly every teenager in America.

Part of the band's appeal came from the fact they were made up of four distinct personalities. Most fans chose a personal favorite among Lennon, McCartney, Harrison and Starr based on how they talked, smiled, or shook their heads while performing.

Beatles' records that had flopped in the U.S. only a year ago now outsold everything else. In April 1964, the Beatles held *all* of five of the top positions on the U.S. singles charts, and twelve of the top one hundred. They also claimed the number one and number two albums. No other musical act has come close to such market domination, before or since. The Beatles would go on to score a record twenty number-one hits, and many of the best-selling albums of all time.

In addition, an unparalleled $50 million was made from various types of merchandise, ranging from bubble gum and trading cards to fuzzy Beatle wigs.

Their fame soon spread throughout the world. They left for a world tour that stretched from Denmark to Australia, where three hundred thousand screaming "Beatlettes," as Lennon now called their female fans, lined the streets of Adelaide as their motorcade passed.

The Beatles took eight weeks off from touring to make a semi-autobiographical movie. The film was called *A Hard Day's Night* after a typical Ringo comment, which the band took to calling "Ringosims," that the drummer uttered after a particularly grueling evening of performing and evading rampant fans. The movie comically looked at the life of the Beatles, as they evaded screaming fans.

The Beatles played to more than 55,000 screaming fans at Shea Stadium in New York. (Courtesy of the Associated Press)

Filled with new songs performed on-screen by the band, it was another success for the group.

Lennon's sudden fame and fortune brought out people from his past, many of whom he thought he'd left behind. His father, Freddie Lennon, appeared in Lennon's life for the first time in twenty years. Back from the sea, Freddie was discovered by the press washing dishes at a London hotel. An awkward reunion was arranged, and Lennon sent him some money with a note that began, "Dear Alf, Fred, Dad, Pater, Father, Whatever . . ."

Freddie insisted that he wanted only parental recognition from his son, though Lennon became skeptical when he sold his story to a magazine and cut a record called, "That's My Life." Over the years, their relationship was rocky and fraught with conflict and distrust. Lennon housed Freddie for a short time but frequently refused to speak to him. His father died in 1976, leaving Lennon again with conflicted feelings toward a father who had deserted him years earlier.

To Lennon and the other Beatles, 1965 sped past in an endless cycle of recording and performing. They had progressed from concert halls to large sports arenas, which they also sold out. In August, the Beatles made history by playing to an audience of more than 55,000 people at New York's Shea Stadium.

Elaborate safeguards had to be set up to protect the foursome at every venue. At Shea Stadium, the stage was placed atop the pitcher's mound, about one hundred feet from the crowded grandstands. The infield was lined with policemen. Shea Stadium Manager Tom Hoving had arranged a safety net in case fans broke through the barrier—the stage was built with a trap door the Beatles could open, then slide down a fireman's pole directly into an armored car.

As the concert began, Hoving feared that this worst-case scenario would occur. "One stroke of the guitar, and you could not hear a single note of music over the screams for the rest of the concert," he reported. "In the first three minutes girls had jumped over the railings out of the stands, and were racing across the baselines. Wc had told the police to restrain the fans without hurting anybody, so there was this bizarre scene of fat New York City cops gently tackling dozens of girls. Somehow it all worked."

Lennon was highly amused by the elaborate security and escapes planned for their appearances. They reminded him of James Bond secret agent movies.

The band tried to maintain a cheery public face. Hoving met them in the Mets' dugout just before they went on.

"They all stood up when I came in, dropped what they were doing and came over. They were just British school-boy polite. I was utterly impressed by their demeanor and behavior; they were really sweet."

Being famous was taking its toll on the band, though. "I never thought I'd run away from attractive young women," marveled Starr, "but by the time they actually get near us, they seem to be completely out of their brains." He, like the other three, had been subjected to crazy exhibitions, ranging from a manic fan ripping from his neck a religious medal he had worn since age ten, to society women clipping locks of his hair as a souvenir.

Because the Beatles could not appear in public without nearly inciting a riot, they were often unable to enjoy the wealth they were quickly acquiring. They felt caged inside hotel rooms and limousines. Publicly, Lennon made light of the situation. When asked, "Would you like to walk down the street without being recognized?" he said, "We used to do this with no money in our pockets. There's no point in it."

In truth, Lennon was dismayed and feeling disconnected from his friends and his fans. Where he once signed autographs gladly for audiences, he was now endlessly pressed with demands from important people or tour employees, many of whom sold the signatures. Sometimes these confrontations were accompanied by snide remarks. Once a British policeman in his motorcade thrust an autograph book through the window and announced, "I see you have the same limousine that you came in last year. Money getting tight then, boys?" Lennon snapped back, "Yeah, and you've got the same bloody uniform on that *you* wore last year. I recognize it."

Lennon began to feel that the Beatles were wearing themselves out playing concerts nobody could hear. At one concert the noise level from continuous screaming of the fans was measured at over 110 decibels, louder than a low-flying jet aircraft. Lennon began mouthing words to songs and strumming air guitar chords when he could no longer hear himself play. "I reckon we could send out four waxwork dummies of ourselves and that would satisfy the crowds," he complained. "Beatles concerts are nothing to do with music any more. They're just bloody tribal rites."

To make matters worse, things sometimes turned violent. Their 1966 world tour included the Philippines, where Imelda Marcos, the wife of the nation's dictator, planned a morning reception for them at her palace before their concert in Manila that afternoon. Nobody had told the band, though, and they were asleep at the hotel when a palace official came to pick them up. They refused to go, and the headline in the next day's *Manila Times* read: "Imelda Stood Up, First Family Waits in Vain for Mopheads."

This was no laughing matter in Marcos' police state. Epstein and the Beatles decided to make a run for the airport but were attacked by military police. Only McCartney escaped being kicked and punched repeatedly as the group ran for the plane.

By the time their tour ended in San Francisco that September, the Beatles were exhausted. It was time for a break from performing.

five

Different Mental Planes

When the 1966 tour was over and the band was returning to Great Britain, Brian Epstein should have been on top of the world. In a few short years he had helped turn the Beatles into the most famous rock 'n' roll band in the world. But Epstein was too worried about his future with the Beatles to be happy. His management contract was set to expire in 1967. Much of his work had been directed toward booking concert dates, and after the chaos of the 1966 tour the band had decided to take a hiatus from touring. He wondered if the band would need him if they no longer toured.

Epstein's relationship with the Beatles had changed. Early on he had been able to exert more control, even over the headstrong John Lennon. But now the power had shifted back to the four musicians. Brian had already been shut out of the music-making process. Lennon had rejected one of Epstein's suggestions during a recording suggestion with the comment, "You stick to your percentages, Brian. We'll make the music." Soon afterward the band and producer George Martin made a firm rule: nobody but necessary recording personnel would be allowed into their recording sessions—no wives, no girlfriends, and no Epstein.

Epstein had always been prone to depression and had fallen into the habit of self-medicating himself with drugs and alcohol. He also had another pressure. He was a homosexual when it was still illegal, at least technically, to engage in homosexual sex in Great Britain.

Many people who spent time around Epstein and the band were convinced he was in love with Lennon. While Lennon acknowledged Epstein as a friend and as a great promoter, his response to the rumors that he might have a homosexual relationship with Epstein was sometimes violent. When a magazine writer accused Lennon of an affair with Epstein at a party, Lennon attacked the writer, sending him to the hospital.

Sometimes, Lennon taunted his manager about both his sexual orientation and his Jewish background. He jokingly referred to Epstein's autobiography, *A Cellar Full of Noise*, as *A Cellar Full of Boys,* or sometimes as *A Cellar Full of Goys.*

It was clear that the relationship between Lennon and Epstein was not good. One of the reasons was Lennon's frustration over Epstein ordering him and the other Beatles not to comment on controversial subjects, such as the increasing U.S. military involvement in Vietnam. By the end of the 1966 tour, Epstein and the Beatles had little personal contact.

Free from touring, the Beatles had to find a way to fill their time. For a short time, Lennon spent time with his family, but soon grew restless. He decided to try acting. He'd already appeared in two movies: *A Hard Day's Night,* and its follow-up *Help!*, another comedy built around Beatles' songs. Richard Lester, who'd directed the Beatles movies, offered Lennon a part in his upcoming film, an antiwar movie titled *How I Won the War.* Lennon jumped at the chance to try a more serious role and settled on a small part playing a character named Private Gripweed. "I feel I want to be them all—painter, writer, actor, singer, player, musician," he said in an interview with *Rolling Stone.*

The part called on him to wear glasses, the same wire rimmed frames he'd hated as a child.

Lennon starred in the 1967 film How I Won the War. (Courtesy of Pictorial Press)

Now older, he liked the look of himself with glasses, and they soon became part of his iconic image.

The film wasn't a success, and most reviewers were lukewarm at best about Lennon as an actor. But it gave him an opportunity to make his position on war clear. He began publicizing his antiwar political views, despite Epstein's command.

In many ways, Lennon was the first of the four band members to let his real personality emerge from the clean young lad image Epstein worked so hard to create. Lennon could not restrain himself from making provocative comments. The first time most of the world was introduced to this side of his personality had come earlier, in the midst of the 1966 U.S. tour, when he had remarked to a British journalist that: "Christianity will go. It will vanish and shrink. I needn't argue about that. I'm right and will be proved right. We're more popular than Jesus now. I don't know which will go first—rock and roll or Christianity."

Conservative Christians in the U. S. were enraged. In Alabama, two thousand teenagers piled hundreds of Beatles records onto a bonfire, and a few dozen radio stations across America banned their songs.

The press began asking Lennon if he truly thought the Beatles were "bigger then Jesus." Lennon tried to explain that he was not blaspheming, but pointing out that Christianity was in such a weakened state that a pop group had a larger following. "I'm not saying that we're better, or greater, or comparing us with Jesus Christ as a person or God as a thing or whatever it is, you know," he explained.

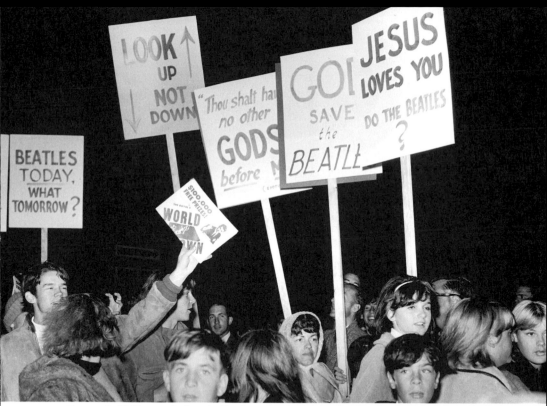

Lennon's 1966 remark that the Beatles were more popular than Jesus sparked a fury of protests from conservative Christians in the United States. (Courtesy of the Associated Press)

"I just said what I said . . . If I had said television is more popular than Jesus, I might have got away with it."

The controversy over the Christianity comment didn't stop Lennon from sharing his opinions about war and politics. If anything, it seemed to encourage him to continue taking public stands. Following *How I Won The War*'s release he said, "I hate war. The Vietnam War and all that is being done there made me feel like that. If there is another war I won't fight—and although the youngsters may be asked to fight I'll stand up there and try to tell them not to. I hate all the sham about war."

Suddenly, Lennon was not just a pop star. He was also a pundit with followers who listened to his every word, and others who began to attack him for his political positions.

Along with the rise of the Beatles in the mid-to late 1960s were other popular British bands, including The Rolling Stones. (Courtesy of the Associated Press)

Few entertainers had ever caused so much controversy because of his political opinions.

Lennon still considered himself to be a musician first. The Beatles had created a new genre of British rock 'n' roll and since 1964 other British bands, such as the Rolling Stones, Dave Clark Five, and their old Liverpool friends Gerry & the Pacemakers, had come to dominate British and U.S. music charts. Many American bands, such as the Byrds, were also clearly influenced by the Beatles. Elvis, Little Richard, Jerry Lee Lewis and others who brought rock 'n' roll to the world ten years earlier now sounded dated.

To ensure they continued sounding fresh, the Beatles

began absorbing new musical influences and working these new sounds into their compositions. Lennon's "Norwegian Wood" was written and performed in a stripped-down style inspired by Bob Dylan, a singer-songwriter who had come out of the American folk tradition, and McCartney embellished his "Elanor Rigby" with an orchestra. Harrison, who was beginning to write songs the band recorded, even incorporated a nineteen-stringed Indian instrument, the sitar, into a few songs.

Unlike their earlier hits, these new songs were more complex and subtle, not suited to being played before thousands of screaming fans. They also had more lyrical depth and ambiguity and demanded more attention from the listener than songs such as "I Want to Hold Your Hand" and "I Saw Her Standing There." This did nothing to slow the sales of Beatles singles and albums, however.

The Beatles had also begun experimenting more widely with drugs. They had taken amphetamines back in their Hamburg days, but as the sixties decade continued, drug use expanded among many parts of the youth culture. American songwriter, Bob Dylan, is credited with introducing the band to marijuana when he visited their New York hotel suite during their U. S. tour. When he asked if they wanted to smoke marijuana, Dylan was surprised to hear that the Beatles had never tried it. "But what about your song," he asked, "the one about getting high?" He was referring to "I Want to Hold Your Hand," and misinterpreting the line "I can't hide," as "I get high."

About a year after first smoking marijuana, the Beatles began to use the hallucinogenic drug LSD. The first time Lennon used LSD he was with Cynthia: it was slipped to them by their dentist during a dinner party. Before long drug use began affecting Lennon and Cynthia's already tense marriage. The drug use separated them, she noted later. "We were on different mental planes. John's thoughts would always be more expansive than mine. I'd seen the effects of drugs and I didn't want to be there. He did. He kept saying that on his trips he was seeing beautiful things."

Many thought the Beatles loaded their album, *Sgt. Pepper's Lonely Hearts Club Band*, with drug references.

The Beatles album, Sgt. Pepper's Lonely Hearts Club Band, *was unlike anything the pop music community had ever seen or heard.* (Courtesy of Pictorial Press)

Lennon countered that he was being misinterpreted again. Although their drug use probably had an impact on everything they did during this period, the biggest influence on *Sgt. Pepper* was a new Beach Boy's album called *Pet Sounds,* particularly its single, "Good Vibrations," which combined beautiful harmonies with the odd sounds produced by an electronic instrument called a theremin.

The Beach Boys was one of the bands and musicians, along with Bob Dylan, the Rolling Stones, the Byrds, and a few others, that sought to rival the Beatles in both creativity and musicality. Beach Boys leader Brian Wilson admitted that *Pet Sounds* was his attempt to raise the bar set by the Beatles' albums *Rubber Soul* and *Revolver.* Lennon, McCartney, Harrison, and Starr in turn felt the pressure from these challengers and wanted to continue making music as different and progressive as *Pet Sounds.*

When they went into the studio to record *Sgt. Pepper* they decided to produce a concept album built around a fictitious ensemble inspired by the Salvation Army bands Lennon had heard at Strawberry Fields as a boy. The first song recorded was Lennon's composition "Strawberry Fields Forever." In it, he tried to recapture the feeling of his early childhood with lyrics that flowed in real-time dialogue, and with music laden with the sounds of an instrument called a mellotron, which could reproduce a huge assortment of taped sounds. The rest of the band and George Martin added elements of their own. "We transformed it into the sort of psychedelic dream, so it was everybody's magical place, instead of just ours," McCartney observed.

This song, and a companion childhood piece written by McCartney, "Penny Lane," were released as a single and left off the album, but they set the tone for subsequent compositions.

Some of the songs were believed to reference drug usage. The BBC banned "Lucy in the Sky with Diamonds" because it was thought to be a code name for LSD. Lennon insisted it was misinterpreted. "My son came home and showed me this drawing of a strange-looking woman flying around," Lennon explained, "and I said, 'What is it?' And he said, 'It's Lucy in the Sky with Diamonds.' It wasn't about LSD at all."

Sgt. Pepper producer Martin backed Lennon up. "Lennon wasn't like that, and people credit him with too much subtlety," Martin points out. "He liked to *shock* people, and if he'd really wanted to write about drugs he would have done it straight out."

Recorded over seven hundred hours, the album broke new ground in rock 'n' roll music with its experimental touches, some of which were purposefully frivolous. After the final song, for example, they recorded themselves playing high-pitched dog whistles. The result was that when people played the album, though they heard nothing after the last song, the dogs would hear the whistles and start barking.

They wanted an iconic cover for the album. All four of the Beatles sported mustaches, were fitted in brightly colored marching band uniforms, and posed with Beatle dummies from Madame Tussaud's Wax Museum in London.

As a final touch they surrounded themselves with dozens of faces of people they would like to see in a crowd. A few of the suggested faces—Lennon wanted to use images of Jesus Christ and Adolf Hitler—were vetoed by the record company, but the end result contained an eclectic group ranging from nineteenth century author Edgar Allan Poe to a doll of 1930s child actress Shirley Temple wearing a Rolling Stones T-shirt. The cover was one of the earliest gatefold designs, which opened to a twenty-five-inch spread of the Beatles. All of the album's lyrics were printed on the back cover.

Sgt. Pepper's Lonely Heart's Club Band, an album unlike any ever seen or heard before, sold almost twelve million copies after its release and won four Grammy Awards in 1967. It remains one of the iconic events in popular music and is credited with forever altering rock music.

Sgt. Pepper was embraced by the newly developing youth culture, particularly those that were coming to be called hippies. Hippie was a journalistic label for the young people that had begun to congregate in San Francisco and other cities. Many took drugs and advocated a more communal society based on peace, love, and freedom from restrictions or interference. Although the Beatles did not let any of the songs on *Sgt. Pepper* be released individually, their next hit single, "All You Need is Love," became a hippie anthem. It was the centerpiece of a BBC television broadcast called "Our World," which was viewed by about four hundred million people, though not shown in the U.S.

Young hippies in San Francisco and other parts of the world were especially enthralled with the Beatles' Sgt. Pepper's Lonely Hearts Club Band *album.* (Courtesy of Pictorial Press)

In spite of the massive success of *Sgt Pepper*, Lennon was unhappy. Specifically, he was not content in his marriage. "There was nothing basically wrong with my marriage to Cyn," Lennon observed. "It was just like an amber light. It wasn't on go and it wasn't on stop. I supposed that me being away so much during the early years of our marriage, I never did feel like the average married man."

He began to feel trapped in the sprawling mansion he had bought in London's suburban stockbroker belt and envied McCartney's bachelor life. McCartney lived in the heart of "Swinging London" and attended private parties and gallery openings almost nightly. Lennon, who had purchased a Rolls Royce and had it painted in psychedelic colors, began slipping away to spend more and more time in London without Cynthia.

One day while in London, Lennon went to a preview of an art exhibition at the Indica gallery, which was co-owned by the brother of McCartney's current girlfriend. There he was introduced to the exhibiting artist, a 33-year-old Japanese woman named Yoko Ono. After they were introduced, Yoko handed Lennon a card, which read, simply, "breathe."

Ono's work was conceptual, which meant it was supposed to trigger an emotion rather than try to be beautiful. In one exhibit she priced an apple at almost $400 to illustrate the absurdity of placing monetary values on objects.

Lennon, always looking for a chance to be cheeky, picked up the apple and said, "Look, I don't have to pay all that money for an apple," and took a bite. Ono was incensed, but held her tongue. She hoped Lennon would become her benefactor. McCartney had already turned her down.

Lennon might have known she wanted him to support her and had decided to have some fun at her expense. After eating the apple, he proceeded to another display, a stepladder. When Ono informed him that it would cost five shillings to climb the ladder and drive an imaginary nail into the wall, Lennon asked, "Suppose I drive an imaginary nail for five *imaginary* shillings?" This won a smile from the usually reserved Ono.

Lennon (center), *along with Cynthia, McCartney, Starr, and Harrison traveled to India to meet with Maharishi and learn meditation.* (Courtesy of Pictorial Press)

Lennon then announced that the event was nutty. Undeterred, Ono began to call his house and to send him postcards with messages such as, "Watch all the lights until dawn." Whether her interest in Lennon was financial support, or had turned into something more romantic at this point was unclear. What was clear was that she was pursuing him. Initially, Cynthia paid Ono little attention. She had grown accustomed to women hurling themselves at her husband. Lennon seemed to be sometimes amused at Ono's antics, and at other times seemed irritated, but couldn't bring himself to end her attention.

Around this same time Lennon and Cynthia accompanied McCartney, Harrison and their girlfriends, to a lecture on transcendental meditation, a mental enlightenment technique from India. Ono also attended the meeting, alone. After the event was over, she climbed into the Lennon's limousine and asked for a ride. Too stunned to refuse, Lennon and Cynthia dropped her off on their way home.

That night, Cynthia asked Lennon about Ono's stalking. "Oh, don't worry about it," Lennon insisted. "It's not that important. Crazy crazy crazy, Cyn! She's another nutter wanting money for all that avant-garde b.s."

Soon after Lennon met Yoko Ono, and was introduced to meditation, Brian Epstein died from a drug overdose. His death threw the band into confusion. Lennon, who had previously resented Brian's rules, began to wonder what they would do without him. "I knew we were in trouble then," Lennon confessed later. "I didn't have any misconceptions about our ability to do anything but play music, and I was scared."

Lennon remained adamantly opposed to going back on tour but wanted to find a way to follow up the success of *Sgt. Pepper.* They finally decided to make another movie. They were under contract to produce a third movie for United Artists, the company that had released *A Hard Day's Night* and *Help!,* and it seemed like a good way to remain in the public eye without touring.

They pondered several ideas, including a film version of the newly popular *Lord of the Rings* books, with each Beatle taking a character. McCartney would play the Hobbit hero Frodo, with Starr as his sidekick Sam. Harrison could be the wise wizard Gandalf, while Lennon would play the creature Gollum. This idea was nixed, however, and they settled on a film about happenings aboard a bewitched Beatles' bus.

As they began the project, there were signs that did not bode well for the future. They were not all in agreement on the idea. Lennon did not care much for it and limited his contribution to a few songs. The film, *Magical Mystery Tour,* never came together. Without Epstein's organization and management, the filming was chaotic. There was barely a plot. It was so poorly received that United Artists refused to accept it as fulfillment of their contract and the Beatles sold it to the BBC for television broadcast.

Magical Mystery Tour was watched by 20 million British people, but it was largely panned by critics. One reviewer said: "'The Magical Mystery Tour is waiting to take you away,' they said, 'but no one is willing to go!'" American TV networks had little interest in the film, and only the addition of previously released singles helped boost the *Magical Mystery Tour* record to number one. The Beatles had suffered their first relative commercial failure (though it developed a cult following over time).

They decided to take a vacation. The peace of mind promised by transcendental meditation, or TM, seemed like the perfect solution to help them escape the pressure of being the world's most famous band. In February 1968, Lennon and Cynthia, along with the other Beatles, wives and girlfriends, traveled to India to study TM under the guru they had met in Britain, Maharishi Mahesh Yogi.

When they arrived at the poor Indian village Maharishi lived in, the Beatles encountered, for the first time in years, people who didn't recognize them—and it was a relief. Although the village was poor, Maharishi's large home had a swimming pool and helicopter pad. It was all paid for by Maharishi's celebrity pupils.

Lennon was pleased to learn that they would be joined at the TM compound by fellow musicians, including Mike Love of the Beach Boys and a popular Scottish singer-songwriter named Donovan. Lennon delighted in playing the entertainer. Donovan recalled that before their first lesson: "We were all wondering what to say. John was so funny and direct that, to break the silence, he went up to the Maharishi, who was sitting cross-legged on the floor, patted him on the head and said, 'There's a good little guru!' We all laughed, it was so funny."

Lennon stopped taking drugs—a Maharishi rule—while at the compound and appeared to eagerly absorb the lessons on the meditative life. TM didn't help his marriage, however. "Every morning he would be up and out of our room before me, at seven o'clock, saying he was off to meditate alone," Cynthia later recalled. "He cut me dead in the mornings . . . I couldn't understand why at the time; I put it down to being away and his changed attitudes to meditation and the beauty that there were now no drugs . . . I realized later that he was going to collect the morning mail with letters from Yoko."

Ono sent almost daily letters to Lennon that were filled with cryptic messages that intrigued him, such as, "I'm a cloud. Watch for me in the sky."

In between meditating, and leisurely playing guitar with the other Beatles, Donovan, and Mike Love, Lennon launched into one of his most fruitful songwriting periods in years. "I was going humity-humity in my head," he said, "and these songs were coming out. For creating, it was great!"

His lyrics, though, betrayed a somewhat darker mental state. One particular line in "Yer Blues" went:

> *Black cloud across my mind, blue mist round my soul*
> *Feel so suicidal, even hate my rock and roll*

After a few months in India, Lennon began to question the Maharishi's motives. The Beatles were frequently being photographed at his side and he heard a rumor that the Maharishi planned to release an album of his lectures and was lining up television appearances to tout himself as the Beatles' spiritual advisor. Angry at being made a part of the Maharishi's publicity campaign, Lennon, Harrison, and their wives—Ringo had already left—prepared to leave. When the Maharishi asked why they were departing, Lennon said, "If you're so bloody cosmic, you'll know why."

The trip was not a complete waste. They returned to England drug free for the first time in months and with thirty new songs, fifteen written by Lennon. Back home, his friend Shotton observed that the only downside to being in India was that he had to part with a week's wages from the millions the Beatles made per year. Lennon laughed. "Actually, Pete," he said, "I never got around to paying him!"

six

Death of the Beatles

When they returned from India, Lennon and the other band members had to find a way to deal with the increasingly complex business side of The Beatles. They had to make decisions that had previously been left to Epstein.

The first thing facing them was a huge tax bill. They were told that unless they quickly invested almost $6 million of their earnings it would be taken in British taxes. The best way to avoid the tax bite was to launch a company as a tax shelter. They decided to call the new company Apple.

From the beginning, they felt that Apple did not have to succeed financially. As Lennon saw it, "It's only money the taxman would have taken anyway." They were free to approach Apple as a creative project. McCartney suggested they start a store that sold only white merchandise. "We could have a department where they sell nothing but white clothes, another where you can buy white furniture—even a white grand piano—and still another where you can buy white pets," he proposed.

McCartney's idea was dropped in favor of opening Apple Boutique that would sell "beautiful things," from custom-designed clothing to hand-painted psychedelic furniture.

Apple soon moved into other businesses, including records, films and television.

In a guest appearance on the U.S. late night show, *Tonight Show*, Lennon laid out Apple's mission: "The aim of the company isn't a stack of gold teeth in the bank. We'd done that bit. It's more of a trick to see if we can get artistic freedom within a business structure; to see if we can create things and sell them without charging three times our cost."

This idealistic approach was hard to turn into reality. They hired four young Dutch designers collectively known as the Fool to create their clothing line and essentially gave them an unlimited budget. Pete Shotton, who managed the boutique, complained to Lennon when one Fool insisted that even the tags of all Apple merchandise be custom woven of pure silk. "From the business angle," Shotton said, "it's sheer insanity. The labels will cost us more to make than most of the actual clothes."

"Oh, just do it the way he wants," Lennon directed. "Remember, Pete, we're not business freaks, we're artists. That's what Apple's all about—artists."

This idealistic rationale did not win over everyone, however. The London neighborhood council forced the Apple Boutique to whitewash its four-story psychedelic exterior paint job. There was also a problem with employee and customer theft. Within months, the boutique was $200,000 in debt.

On July 31, 1968, Lennon and McCartney closed the store, but in typically grand style. The first customer that

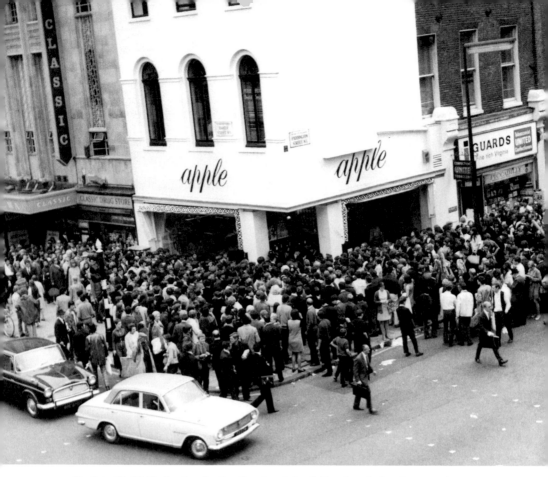

On July 31, 1968, the day the Beatles closed Apple Boutique in London, a mob quickly gathered at the store when word spread that the Fab Four were giving the merchandise away. (Courtesy of John Roddgers/Redferns)

day at the Apple Boutique was informed that his purchase would be free. Word flew, and a mob quickly picked the store clean, even taking the hangars and fixtures. Lennon and McCartney applauded their happening, but sobered when they learned that more than $40,000 in goods they gave away were fully taxable under British law.

Apple Records was not much more successful. They ran an ad inviting anyone to submit a tape and within weeks were inundated with more than 40,000 submissions, most of which were never played. Artists they did sign, such as

American James Taylor, left the label because they were not getting enough attention. Televisions, electric typewriters, cases of wine, even gold albums commemorating top-selling Beatles' records vanished. Three company cars disappeared.

At the same time the Apple experiment was descending into chaos, Lennon's personal life was also in turmoil. Yoko Ono was now a large part of Lennon's life. Although he had dismissed her as a "nutter" to Cynthia, he had given Ono about $9,000 to fund a new art exhibit. Lennon avoided the show and insisted on not being identified as its benefactor. The collection cryptically bore the subtitle "Yoko and Me."

As Lennon became more intrigued by Ono, his marriage to Cynthia deteriorated. Though Lennon bemoaned his lack of privacy while on tour, he found it difficult to transition from public adulation to being a full-time husband and father when off the road. He was increasingly indifferent to Cynthia and impatient with Julian. He preferred going to parties and spending time with creative people to being at home with his wife and son.

Cynthia had little interest in parties and drugs but Ono was a fixture at the parties Lennon attended. Separated from her own husband, she was clearly pursuing Lennon. One night, while Cynthia and Julian were vacationing in Greece, he called her and invited her to his house. Once she got there, Lennon later reported:

> I didn't know what to do. So we went upstairs to my studio and I played her all the tapes that I'd made of this far-out stuff,

some comedy stuff, some electronic music. She was suitably impressed and said, 'Well, let's make one ourselves.' So we made *Two Virgins*, and it was dawn when we finished. And then we made love at dawn. It was very beautiful.

Cynthia returned the next day to find the couple sitting at the kitchen table in bathrobes. Cynthia later said, "I suppose I should have been prepared for it, but I wasn't. It took my breath away. I wasn't angry. I was just absolutely shattered at the vision . . . I decided John had been almost willing me to go. I took his silence as saying, 'Don't interrupt this fantastic situation. Get lost. You're spoiling things.'"

Lennon left his wife, Cynthia, when his affair with Yoko Ono was revealed in 1968. The two quickly began imitating one another with their long, parted hairstyles and all-white outfits. (Courtesy of Andrew Maclear/Redferns)

As Lennon and Cynthia began divorce proceedings, Ono was always at his side. His friends joked that she was surgically implanted and that they had come to resemble twins when Lennon grew his hair longer and parted it in the middle like Ono, and both wore all white clothes.

Lennon's image was changing in other ways. Over the years he had given up wearing suits in favor of colorful shirts and bellbottom pants, and he had begun wearing his once-hated granny glasses. Without Brian Epstein crafting his image, Lennon was free to present himself to the media however he pleased, and the press, and the public, didn't always like what they saw.

His quick divorce and even quicker taking up with Ono shocked many people. The press began asking more confrontational questions, such as, "Where's your wife? Where's Cynthia? What happened to your wife, John?" When Ono became pregnant—while both of them were still married to other people—the questions grew even more aggressive. Many Beatles' fans shared the press's scorn. Even Aunt Mimi was not supportive. When she first met Ono, she reportedly asked, "Who's the poison dwarf, John?"

Lennon claimed to not understand why people were so upset about his affair with Ono. He was clearly so deeply infatuated with her and the life they had started together that he referred to them simply as JohnandYoko, and seemed to care little for what anyone else thought.

The lovebirds were pressured from other quarters. In October 1968, the police raided an apartment Lennon and Ono were staying in, and a small quantity of hashish was found. Lennon denied that the drug belonged to them, and pointed out that Starr owned the flat. But they were found guilty and fined about $300.

Although he denied that the hashish was his, Lennon and Ono were using drugs together, including heroin. Lennon rationalized their use of the dangerous drug as a way to escape the contempt being heaped on them by the press. He explained that when using hcroin, "I felt like a baby wrapped in cotton wool and floating on warm water."

1968 continued to be a challenging year. In November, Ono miscarried their baby. In the hospital, Lennon recorded the fetus's final heartbeats and rarely left her side for three weeks, sleeping on a mattress on the floor, as she recovered.

Lennon and Ono's relationship exacerbated a rift that had developed within the Beatles. "As soon as I met her, that was the end of the boys," he later observed, "but it so happened that the boys were well-known and weren't just the local guys at the bar."

The other Beatles had been fond of Cynthia. When she and John separated, McCartney offered Cynthia his support. He felt so sad for their son Julian, he wrote a song for him entitled "Hey Jules" with the line: "Hey Jules, don't make it bad, take a sad song and make it better. . . ." Eventually, the name was changed to "Hey Jude."

Creative tensions in the band were at a high point. In the past, this tension had been part of their success. Lennon and McCartney's different approaches to music had helped them forge their distinctive sound. McCartney had a gift for beautiful melodies and leaned toward ballads and other songs that sometimes slipped into sentimentality. Lennon's music remained more hard-edged and angry. He had also begun experimenting with different sounds and instruments and including political and social messages in some of his compositions. In the early years the two were often able to balance one another's tendencies, but by 1968 they were writing fewer songs together and their different approaches were becoming more pronounced and incompatible.

Harrison, meanwhile, was growing as a songwriter in his own right, and felt that more of his songs should be included on the albums. Previously, albums had yielded only one or two spots for Harrison's compositions. Starr was also composing, but he was largely content playing drums and singing the occasional Lennon/McCartney composition.

Lennon exacerbated tensions, and violated a long-standing agreement to not bring outsiders to recording sessions, when

1968

The 1960s were a turbulent decade in many parts of the world, and 1968 has come to be seen as the climactic year. That spring, students and workers rioted against the government of Charles de Gaulle in France and Soviet troops invaded Czechoslovakia to prop up the teetering communist dictatorship.

The year started with the Tet Offensive in January when North Vietnamese and Viet Cong guerrilla fighters launched a series of surprise attacks against U. S. and South Vietnam forces throughout South Vietnam. Although the North Vietnamese and Viet Cong were defeated and their onslaught stopped, their ability to attack in the heart of Saigon, the South Vietnamese capital, and wage a fierce battle surprised many in the U. S. government and shocked citizens at home who had hoped the war would end soon. Some historians today consider the Tet Offensive to be the turning point in the war, which led to eventual U. S. withdrawal and the North Vietnamese victory.

1968 was also a violent year. In the U. S. the protests against the Vietnam War often became violent and in London an antiwar demonstrations turned into a conflict with the police that left ninety-one police officers injured, and more than two hundred protesters, mostly students, were arrested. In April, student protesters at New York's Columbia University seized several administration buildings and shut down the university for about a week. Most famously, protesters, led by the Chicago Seven (including Jerry Rubin and Abbie Hoffman) clashed with police outside the Democratic National Convention that summer.

The on-going struggle for civil rights for African Americans had suffered a series of violent attacks by those opposed to the end of racial segregation. A protest that year at a whites-only bowling alley in South Carolina led to the deaths of three college students, for example. But the most traumatic act of racial violence of 1968 occurred on April 4, when civil rights leader Martin Luther King Jr. was assassinated in Memphis, Tennessee. Riots erupted in many U.S. cities in the days after King was murdered.

Two months later, on the evening of June 5, Democratic Presidential candidate Robert Kennedy, brother of assassinated president John F. Kennedy, was assassinated by Sirhan Sirhan on the very night he had won the California primary. That November, Republican Richard Nixon was elected president. In his campaign Nixon had promised to continue the Vietnam War, which insured that the violence that characterized 1968 would continue into the next decade.

he began showing up with Ono. Although she had previously claimed no interest in popular music, Ono soon began giving unsolicited advice to the group. "That was a bit difficult to deal with," said producer George Martin. "Suddenly she would appear in the control room. Nobody would say anything to me. I wasn't even introduced to her; she would just sit there. And her influence could be felt. To begin with, everyone was *irritated* by her." She even went so far as to have a bed installed in the studio, with a mike near her pillow so she could comment while reclining.

Regardless of what they thought of him bringing Ono to the studio, Lennon was most appalled by how his closest friends treated his new love. "They insulted her," he said later. McCartney later said that he "hated Yoko," and didn't grow to like her until much later. Other members of the entourage simply ignored her, a slight that only further aggravated Lennon. According to him, only Ringo Starr and his then-wife Maureen were friendly to the new couple.

Ono's presence was just one of many problems plaguing the band. The issue of their increased productivity was also becoming a problem. As Lennon and McCartney were now doing most of their writing separately, and Harrison was demanding more space for his songs, the Beatles realized a traditional album wouldn't be big enough to hold all the music they had written.

To solve this problem, they decided their next release would be a double album. But even an expanded album wasn't large enough for all of the songs they wanted to include, and they bickered over what would make the cut. The usually congenial Starr got so frustrated he stormed out of the sessions and refused to return for two weeks.

Eventually they were able to agree on which songs to include, but to avoid getting into more arguments about the album's cover they also agreed to not have any artwork on the cover. Instead, they released it in a white sleeve only. The double album was titled simply *The Beatles,* but became better known as the *White Album.*

Lennon's compositions on the new album increasingly dealt with personal subjects. "Sexy Sadie," for example, vented his disillusionment at the Maharishi (Lennon later admitted that the song was in fact about the Maharishi, but he copped out and didn't directly address the unscrupulous guru):

> *Sexy Sadie, what have you done?*
> *You made a fool of everyone.*

One of Lennon's most personal new songs was "Julia." Borrowing passages from Arab poet Kahil Gibran's *The Prophet*, the song expressed longing for his mother, Julia, and for Ono, referred to as "ocean child," the English translation of her name. It was the first song Lennon recorded with no other Beatles involved. "Bungalow Bill," on the other hand, about an odd family he met in India, involved everyone, including Ono. Her voice marked the first appearance by a woman on any Beatles recording.

Another notable song was the politically charged "Revolution." By late 1968, demand for change in society had shifted from the nonbelligerent flower power of the Summer of Love to talk of overthrowing the governments of world powers such as the United States and Britain, violently if necessary. Radicals were certain the politically opinionated Lennon would support their cause, but they had always misunderstood him. He had lobbied for peace, not for violently overthrowing an entire social order, and he made this clear in "Revolution" with lyrics like:

> *But when you talk about destruction*
> *Don't you know you can count me out?*

Newspapers such as New York's *Village Voice* criticized Lennon for opposing the proper line. He responded, "I'm [now] not only up against the establishment, but you too. I'll tell you what's wrong with the world: people. So do you want to destroy them? Until you/we change our heads, there's no chance. Tell me of one successful revolution."

Lennon was pleased with "Revolution." It was written and recorded in a direct rock style that eschewed the more baroque arrangements on *Sgt. Pepper*. As such, it reminded Lennon of the classic rock and roll that had inspired him to start making music as a youth.

"Revolution" was intended to be the next Beatles single, until McCartney debuted "Hey Jude." After debating which song would be released, they reached a compromise, though McCartney got the edge because the consensus was that "Hey Jude" had more commercial potential. His song appeared on the "A" side of the record, with "Revolution" on the "B" side, in what many consider the strongest two-sided single ever issued. Both songs received heavy airplay, and the single eventually sold about ten million copies worldwide, fifth on the all-time best-seller list. The *White Album* ranks sixth on the all-time album list with sales of 19 million copies.

Despite the band's continued success, Lennon, along with Harrison and Starr, were, "fed up with being sidemen for Paul. After Brian died, that's what began to happen to us." He longed to create something more personal and idiosyncratic, something with Ono. They decided to release the collection of sound clips from their first night together. Called *Two Virgins*, the album's art consisted of frontal and rears pictures of Lennon and Ono, totally naked.

Lennon admitted that, "I want people to be shocked." As expected, the cover met resistance from EMI, which manufactured Beatles records in Britain. Lennon and Ono took their case to EMI Chairman Sir Joseph Lockwood. "Well, aren't you shocked?" Lennon asked.

"No, I've seen worse than this," Lockwood said.

"So it's all right then, is it?" Lennon asked.

"No, it's *not* alright," replied Lockwood. "I'm not worried about the rich people, the duchesses, and those people who follow you. But your mums and dads and girl fans will object strongly. You will be damaged, and what will you gain? What's the purpose of it?"

"It's art," Ono answered.

"Well," Lockwood retorted, "I should find some better bodies to put on the cover than your two. They're not very attractive. Paul McCartney would look better naked than you."

Dead Paul

A good indication of how popular the Beatles were during the 1960s, and their hold over the imagination of young people all over the globe, occurred in the spring of 1969 when millions of fans were convinced that Paul McCartney was actually dead and that there had been an immense conspiracy to cover up his death.

The phenomenon began in May when a Detroit based songwriter named Terry Knight had a regional hit in the Midwestern U. S. with a song called "Saint Paul." Lyrics in the song referred to Paul McCartney being in heaven. Soon after the song was released an article appeared in an Iowa student newspaper that claimed Paul McCartney was dead and citing the song as evidence. A few weeks later, Detroit radio DJ named Russ Gibb took a call from a caller who outlined on air the points made in the student newspaper. One of the points was that if the song "Revolution Number 9" from the so-called *White Album* was played backwards the words "Turn me on, dead man" could clearly be heard.

A student journalist at the University of Michigan heard this broadcast and wrote his own article claiming that McCartney was dead and detailing numerous other obscure clues from Beatles' album covers and lyrics. Soon rumors that Paul McCartney was dead and had been replaced by a lookalike had created a firestorm.

The story that eventually developed was that after McCartney had left a recording session on November 9, 1966 and was driving home he had a horrific car crash. His body had been severely burned, and his head was crushed, which rendered his body unidentifiable. Rather than risk alienating their fans at the height of their popularity, the remaining Beatles had held an innocent "Paul McCartney Look-Alike-Contest." The winner was a Canadian named William Campbell, who was then given plastic surgery to make him look even more like Paul, although a telltale scar had been left near his lip.

After successfully pulling off the substitution, the remaining Beatles, wracked with guilt about duping the public and hiding their friend's death, had begun to insert clues into Beatles artwork and lyrics that revealed the truth. Several of the clues could be found in the cover art of *Sergeant Pepper's Lonely Hearts Club Band.* Fans found that if one used a mirror to bisect the phrase "Lonely Hearts" on the drum set, it reads: "I ONE IX HE   DIE" that was further decoded to read "11 9 HE DIE," a reference to supposed date of Paul's death. The floral arrangement at the foreground of the photo was interpreted to be a funeral wreath, and the yellow flowers in the bottom right seem to be in the shape of a bass guitar and spelled out "Paul?" McCartney is also the only person holding a black instrument, black being a funereal color associated with death, and on the back of the album McCartney is the only one facing backwards. The words "Without You," from the lyric sheet, are right next to McCartney's head. There is also a raised hand with an open palm above McCartney's head. It was claimed the open palm is a symbol of death in some cultures. Furthermore, some point out that the open palm can be seen in many pictures of McCartney.

The cover of *Abbey Road* is often interpreted as a funeral procession for Paul. Lennon, dressed in white, is the priest, Starr, dress in black, is the undertaker, and Harrison, wearing denim, is the gravedigger. McCartney, in the middle of the group, isn't wearing shoes, a supposed reference to the fact that corpses are sometimes buried without shoes. McCartney is also shoeless in various photos found in the booklet that came with the *Magical Mystery Tour* album. Fans have also noted that in the picture that left-handed McCartney is holding his cigarette in his right hand. On the cover of *Let It Be*, all of the Beatles except McCartney are facing to the left, in front of a light colored background. McCartney is facing forward, in front of a blood-red background. Others pointed out that in photos of the band, starting with the *Sgt. Pepper* cover, McCartney appears to be about two inches taller than he was in previous photos.

There are also numerous supposed lyrical clues. In addition to the aforementioned reference on "Revolution, Number 9," some said they can hear Lennon saying "I buried Paul" at the end of "Strawberry Fields Forever." Lennon later pointed out that he was saying "cranberry sauce." Lennon's "A Day in the Life" features the lyrics "he blew his mind out in a car, he didn't notice that the lights had changed," which some interpret as being a recounting of McCartney's fatal road accident.

These are only a few of the clues devoted fans found. Some even found clues in albums made before McCartney's supposed death. Not surprisingly, McCartney denied being dead. However, there had been a car crash in January 1967 involving McCartney's car—but he wasn't in it at the time. He also was involved in a moped accident in 1966, from which he received the small scar on his lip.

There is still some debate over whether this was an intentional hoax by the band, or just the product of overly eager fans. All of the band members claimed that it wasn't planned; however, during the peak of the "Paul is dead" rumors in 1969, sales of Beatles albums did drastically increase. And nobody ever explained why McCartney was suddenly taller . . .

Despite their hesitations, EMI eventually agreed to press some copies of *Two Virgins*, but Apple would have to handle all distribution and marketing. When the first copies were shipped to the U.S. they were confiscated by customs officials and prohibited from sale under obscenity laws. They ultimately had to be sold in brown wrappers and even then most stores refused to carry the album. Instead of establishing JohnandYoko as artists distinct from the Beatles, *Two Virgins* only magnified public disapproval of their lives.

By the beginning of 1969, the Beatles were a fractured band, tired of playing together after eleven years, and being pulled apart by personal and financial disagreements. McCartney claimed to want to hold the band together and suggested making a film to document the rehearsals for their next album, which he said could be a live performance in an exotic location such as the Roman Colosseum or Africa's Sahara Desert. When he heard McCartney's idea Lennon quipped, "I'm warming to the idea of an asylum."

A concert film would be a Beatles first, and would finally satisfy their United Artists contract that called for a third film and soundtrack album. (A successful animated film called *Yellow Submarine* didn't qualify because it contained cartoon Beatles instead of the real ones.)

But the Beatles couldn't mask the problems they now had playing together, and the cameras brought in for the concert film project recorded the disintegration of the band. Because the concept was to capture live tracks recorded on the spot and not overdubbed, the Beatles went through dozens of takes of each song, trying to get them right. Tensions were high, and the sessions were filled with unspoken suspicions and accusations. Lennon felt that as McCartney sang, "Get back to where you once belonged," on the single "Get Back," he was addressing Ono. Harrison felt that the band and producer George Martin didn't respect his writing or his guitar playing, and like Starr the year before, he walked out and had to be convinced to return. McCartney, meanwhile, infuriated Lennon by inviting his new girlfriend, Linda Eastman, to the sessions, just as Lennon had done with Ono.

After a month of arguing, the notion of the Beatles traveling anywhere to perform together was out of the question. They decided to perform their concert on the roof of the Apple Records building. On January 30, traffic stopped for blocks around as the Beatles played live for the first time in more than two years. The concert lasted only forty-two minutes before police stopped it when some neighborhood banking executives complained the commotion had stopped their business. As the concert was stopped, Lennon said, "I'd like to say thanks on behalf of the group and ourselves—and I hope we passed the audition."

The rooftop concert was a success, but the recording session had been a fiasco that generated hundreds of hours of audiotape and film that nobody wanted to touch, least of all the Beatles. George Martin backed out of trying to get the tapes into some kind of releasable condition, and when a second producer gave up in frustration, both tape and film sat unedited.

Martin was surprised when McCartney called him a few months later saying the Beatles wanted to cut another album. Despondent as they were about playing together, no one wanted the band to end on such a sour note.

Returning to the studio, Martin insisted on a professional effort, and he received it. There was still a large amount of resentment between the musicians, though, and after they arranged and prepared the songs, they recorded most of their parts individually. It was left to Martin to piece the parts together, and create the effect of a unified group.

Harrison contributed two of the album's best-known songs, "Something" and "Here Comes the Sun." A medley of unfinished song bits was edited together on the album's second side. The final track was "The End." Beginning with Starr's only drum solo on record and progressing through individual guitar licks by Lennon, McCartney and Harrison, the song's only lyric was:

> *And in the end, the love you take*
> *Is equal to the love you make.*

They named the album *Abbey Road*, after the recording studio where they worked.

In August, cult leader Charles Manson led his followers on a killing spree in California. He claimed that he received a directive from "Helter Skelter," a song from the *White Album*, to rise and destroy the world by inciting a race war. Lennon was summoned as a witness for Manson's trial, but refused to testify. He said that "Helter Skelter" was not a call for Armageddon as Manson had interpreted, but the British name for a seesaw. More importantly, even though the controversy centered on Lennon, the song was actually written by McCartney.

The ongoing controversy, and the exhaustion of playing together for more almost a decade, led to worse tensions in the band than ever. Furthermore, each of the band members was moving in different directions. McCartney, Harrison, and Starr had solo albums in the works, and Lennon was in the process of recording an album with Ono.

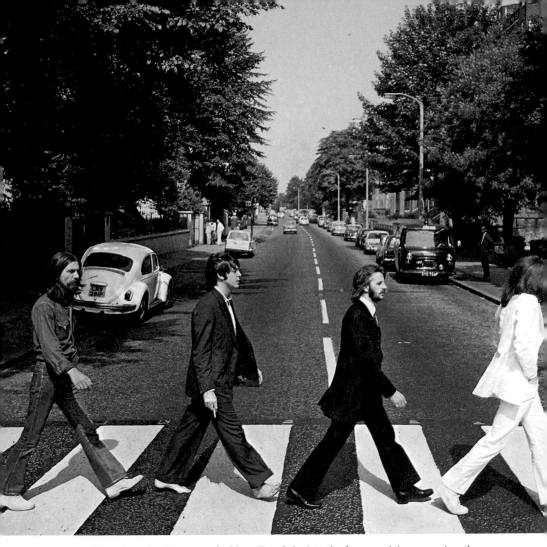

The photo for the cover of Abbey Road *depicts the four musicians crossing the street in front of their recording studio.* (Courtesy of Pictorial Press)

The worst toll on the group, though, was taken by continued disagreement over the future of their finances. Partially as a result of Brian Epstein's inexperience with managing, many of the contracts they had signed took advantage of the then-naïve musicians. Despite being the most successful band in the world, many of their deals hadn't been updated since they began and provided them only nominal royalties and fees. Agents and accountants were getting more than half of the Beatles' profits. Furthermore, though Apple had been set up as a tax shelter, the company's intricate finances made it so that the band members were actually in debt to the company. Little had changed after Epstein's death, when management of their finances fell to Epstein's brother, Clive.

McCartney asked Linda Eastman's father to look into the Beatles' finances. He was particularly interested in acquiring the publishing rights to the Lennon/McCartney compositions that were then owned by Northern Songs Ltd., whose owner was taking in more than half of the proceeds from publishing the songs. Linda's father, Lee Eastman, a New York attorney, sent his son, John Eastman, to serve as the Beatles lawyer, and eventually, take over as manager.

Lennon was wary of putting the future of his band into the hands of Paul's future brother-in-law, as were Harrison and Starr. Lennon set out to find new management for the group and was soon contacted by Allen Klein. Klein was a U.S. accountant who already had experience managing The Rolling Stones, The Kinks, and Donovan, and had been expressing an interest in managing the Beatles since Epstein's death.

With a reputation as a brash and ruthless dealmaker, Klein was distrusted in the British media. He, however, impressed Lennon. Defiant in his attitude, and typically dressed in casual clothes and sneakers, he was the opposite of the posh, upper-class Eastmans. Lennon found Klein to be a kindred spirit. Klein further impressed Lennon with an intimate knowledge of Lennon's work. On their first meeting, they discussed Beatles songs, and Klein knew precisely which parts Lennon had written, although everything was credited to Lennon/McCartney. The Eastmans, on the other hand, treated Lennon as a lucky bloke who had attached himself to McCartney and was along for the ride.

Most importantly, Klein treated Ono with respect. While others, including Lennon's bandmates, tended to ignore Ono or condescend to her, Klein treated her as an equal. Lennon said later about Klein, "[The others] were animals. Allen was a human being. The same as Brian was a human being . . . I make a lot of mistakes character wise. But now and then I make . . . a good one, and Allen's one."

Harrison and Starr agreed that Klein should assume management duties, but McCartney insisted on the Eastmans. A meeting was set up between Klein, the band, and John Eastman. The meeting wasn't a success. The snobby Eastman

The Beatles hired Allen Klein (left) to manage the group after the death of Brian Epstein. (Courtesy of Pictorial Press)

despised the self-made Klein, and treated him with the same patronizing attitude that he used on everyone except McCartney. When Klein revealed that the proud Eastmans had legally changed their name from Epstein to hide their Jewish heritage, Eastman began shouting and insulting Klein, and accused Klein of being a con-man because he had been in trouble with the IRS years earlier.

Lennon, appalled at how his new friend was being treated, denounced Eastman, which angered McCartney. But McCartney, perhaps to appease his bandmates, agreed to allow Klein to look into their finances, though he retained the Eastmans as his personal legal representatives.

Klein spent two months at the Apple offices examining contracts and financial records and discovered their dire financial straits. For example, the group's net income was just 78,000 pounds after various accountants and third parties took their share. Furthermore, Lennon and McCartney were both in debt to Apple for more than 60,000 pounds, and Harrison and Starr were in debt for about 30,000 pounds each. The most successful band in the world was on the verge of bankruptcy.

Klein set to work. He first tried to free the band from their contract with NEMS, Epstein's company, because the company was no longer doing anything for them but was still taking 25 percent of their income. He planned to sue Clive Epstein, but Clive quickly sold the company to Triumph Trust, a much larger company with the resources to fight off Klein's legal challenges. Meanwhile, the heads of Northern Songs, which controlled the publishing rights to the Beatles' songs, sold their share of the company to the Associated Television Corporation (ATV). Suddenly, a major corporation controlled the largest portion of the Beatles' song rights. By September 1969, ATV owned more than 50 percent of the Beatles' publishing rights, while Lennon and McCartney together only owned about 35 percent.

Klein did succeed in buying out their contract from NEMS and Triumph Trust, and the band, in a vote of three to one, with McCartney the dissenting vote, chose to hire Klein as their new manager. Klein negotiated a higher percentage of royalties from every album sold and created a system in which Apple controlled the Beatles' output in a licensing deal with the major record companies such as Capitol and EMI. This gave the band control of their music, though their publishing rights remained owned by ATV until 1986, when they were purchased by pop star Michael Jackson for $47.5 million.

Though Klein was able to salvage the Beatles finances, the dispute between him and Eastman exacerbated the dispute between Lennon and McCartney. Furthermore, Lennon was more enraged when he found out McCartney had delayed the resolution with ATV that might have helped secure their rights to the Beatles' catalog at Eastman's urging.

By 1970, the only time The Beatles spent together was to discuss Apple and their business concerns. McCartney, who still said he wanted to keep the band together, said, "Let's get back to square one and remember what we're all about." He again suggested a Beatles concert in an ancient amphitheater, or as the house band on a worldwide cruise, or a tour of small clubs that would take them back to their beginnings. Lennon responded: "I think you're daft. I wasn't going to tell you but I'm breaking the group up. It feels good. It feels like a divorce." McCartney was disappointed, but not shocked. He later said:

> Looking back, it was largely that John needed a new direction that he went into headlong, helter skelter. He went right in there and did all sorts of stuff he had never done before, with Yoko. And you can't blame him because he was that kind of guy. He wanted to live life, do stuff and there was no holding back with John. And that was what we admired him for. So we couldn't really say: "Oh, we don't want you to do that, John. Stay with us." You'd feel so wimpy. It had to happen.

Even as the band was breaking up, the members, at Klein's urging, decided to keep the news under wraps, at least temporarily. The legendary producer Phil Spector, had "worked like a pig" to patch their failed live album project into an album called *Let it Be*. The film was being put together as well. They agreed to withhold the breakup to keep from sabotaging *Let it Be*'s sales.

Then, two weeks before the scheduled release of *Let it Be*, McCartney released his first solo album and announced that *he* was quitting the Beatles. Lennon was enraged. Not only at McCartney's breaking their vow of silence, but because he felt that the band was his—not McCartney's—to break up. "Paul hasn't left," Lennon responded. "I sacked him."

seven

JohnandYoko

During the chaotic period of the Beatles disintegration, Lennon decided to marry Ono. "We are two love birds," he said. "Intellectually we didn't believe in getting married. But one doesn't love someone just intellectually. For two people, marriage still has the edge over living together."

Ono approached the wedding as though it were an art project. "We're going to stage many happenings, and this wedding is going to be one of them," she said.

The couple flew to the British island of Gibraltar, where they were married in a civil ceremony, and departed the island within an hour after the ceremony. Both bride and groom wore white. They legally took each other's surnames, becoming the Ono-Lennons.

After their wedding, the Ono-Lennons invited the press to their hotel room where they held a "Bed-in For Peace." (Courtesy of Pictorial Press)

For their honeymoon, the Ono-Lennons invited the press to their hotel room in Holland to witness what they called a "Bed-In For Peace." They told reporters that they planned to remain in bed for six days, during which they discussed peace with about one hundred reporters.

"The press would have found us whatever we'd done for a honeymoon," Lennon later reasoned, "so we decided to invite the press along and get some publicity for something we both believe in . . . We are willing to become the world's clowns if it helps spread the word for peace. Too many people talk about it but not enough do anything."

They planned another Bed-In to be held in New York City to protest the U.S. involvement in Vietnam, but Lennon

President Richard Nixon used his influence to keep John Lennon out of the United States because of Lennon's stance against the Vietnam War. (Library of Congress)

was denied a visa. Ostensibly, the visa was denied because of his 1968 drug conviction, but it was later revealed that the real reason was the Nixon Administration's desire to keep an influential antiwar protester out of the country. John and Yoko went to Montreal instead, where they conducted hundreds of phone interviews with U.S. journalists and disc jockeys. They even called leaders of an antiwar riot in California, trying to dissuade both the students and the police from using violence.

During interviews Lennon candidly acknowledged his proclivity towards violence in the past: "It is the most violent people who go in for love and peace . . . I am a violent man who has learned not to be violent and regrets his violence . . . I prefer myself when I'm non-violent."

An assortment of people, including LSD guru Timothy Leary, beat poet Allen Ginsberg, and comedians Tommy Smothers and Dick Gregory joined the Ono-Lennons Montreal Bed-In. During the event Lennon recruited people from all walks of life, including hotel staff and worshipers from a local Krishna temple, to help him record a new song called "Give Peace a Chance." The song, built around of chorus of "all we are saying, is give peace a chance" struck a chord with the public. It charted as high as number two in Britain, and its chorus was adopted as a rallying cry by the anti-Vietnam War movement.

Lennon and Ono continued their very public activism, occasionally staging events that bordered on being ludicrous. Some critics began calling them "Joko," especially when they unveiled their concept of "Bagism" at a press conference in Vienna. The media arrived to find a large white bag concealing Lennon and Ono. Lennon explained the meaning of the display: "If we, or anybody, has something to say, they can communicate from one room to another and not confuse you with what color their skin is, how

long their hair's grown, or how many pimples they've got
. . . It's only what we *say* that's important."

In light of Lennon's increasingly eccentric behavior, some
people came to believe he had caved in to his wife's will.
His closeness and apparent obedience to Yoko did reveal
a side of his character most of the public had not seen
before. Contrary to his apparent independent, rebellious
personality, symbolized most clearly in his proclivity for
controversial statements, Lennon had always been depen-
dent on close companions, such as Brian Epstein, to guide
him. This was a role Ono relished. She said later, "I think
that I was probably the successor to Aunt Mimi." Even
Pete Shotton, who had a prickly relationship with Ono,
conceded, "she enabled the child in John to resurface—the
child I had known and loved. You might almost say that
Yoko brought John back to life."

By 1969 Lennon had not performed live since 1966—and
not without McCartney and Harrison in twelve years. When
he heard that a promoter in Toronto, Canada was organiz-
ing a "Rock and Roll Revival," combining 1950s pioneers
such as Chuck Berry and Little Richard, with current acts
such as the Doors and Alice Cooper, Lennon decided at the
last minute that he wanted to be part of it. He assembled a
band in one day that included Eric Clapton and Ono.

Lennon threw up just before his set. He was seized with
stage fright at the thought of playing before ten thousand
people without the Beatles. He began his set by playing
Elvis Presley's "Blue Suede Shoes" and ended with "Give
Peace a Chance," and said "I can't remember when I've

had such a good time" as he left the stage. He had been a success. Then Ono, who had been mostly rolling around the stage in a duffel bag during Lennon's performance, emerged and performed almost twenty minutes of impassioned caterwauling. The performance was recorded for the album *Live Peace in Toronto.*

Shortly after the performance, Lennon released a single called "Cold Turkey." With guitar played by his friend Eric Clapton, the song documented withdrawal from heroin:

Temperature's rising, fever is high, can't see no future, can't see no sky,
Feet are so heavy, so is my head, I wish I was a baby, I wish I was dead.

The song was recorded during the *Abbey Road* sessions, but McCartney insisted it be kept it off the album. In response to this slight, for the first time since 1957 Lennon released a song with a credit that read "Lennon" without the accompanying "McCartney." Even "Give Peace a Chance," which had been recorded during a Bed-In, was credited to Lennon/McCartney.

"Cold Turkey," with its dark and confessional lyrics, came partially out of Lennon's interest in primal therapy. One of many pop psychologies that flourished in the 1970s, primal therapy encouraged patients to unleash their emotional pain in childlike outbursts, such as a scream. With their usual fervor, Lennon and Ono flew the developer of the therapy, Arthur Janov, to their new seventy-two-acre

British home for several weeks of private sessions. When Janov left, they took advantage of the U. S. visa that had recently been issued to Lennon, and followed him to his clinic in California.

Primal therapy had an influence on the couple's new album, *John Lennon/Plastic Ono Band.* Lennon explained that Janov, "showed me how to feel my own fear and pain, so I could handle it better than I could before." His autobiographical songs increasingly dealt with deeply personal issues that he might have been previously afraid to discuss so publicly. "Mother" in particular emphasized this new trend. Unlike the earlier ode "Julia," "Mother" was a cry out to the parents that had abandoned him and ended with a shout of, "Mommy don't go! Daddy come home!" As a young man, he'd been unable to even talk about his feelings about his mother, but now he was sharing his pain with the world.

On another song he sang a list of things he didn't believe in, ranging from magic to the Beatles, concluding with,

> *I just believe in me; and that's reality . . . I was the Walrus, but now I'm John,*
> *And so dear friends, you'll just have to carry on, the dream is over.*

The song "Working Class Hero" was seen by some who knew him as pretentious because Lennon had actually been raised in more affluence than the other three

Beatles. Nobody was more offended than Aunt Mimi, who had worked hard to provide him opportunities.

John Lennon/Plastic Ono Band climbed to number six on the U.S. charts, the best result to date for a Lennon album, and was generally liked by critics. Nevertheless, Lennon was in the midst of an angry period. He was constantly approached by people who wanted to talk about the Beatles and pleas for them to get back together. He was also tormented by the refusal of the media, and his friends, to accept his marriage to Ono. Most blamed her for the breakup of the Beatles, and for the new, less mainstream direction Lennon was taking with his life and art. There was also a large amount of barely veiled racism directed toward her Japanese heritage and their interracial marriage. In 1970, *Esquire* magazine ran an article entitled "John Rennon's Excrusive Gloupie" that was accompanied by a full page drawing of a hideous Ono, with Lennon as a tiny beetle on a leash.

In an interview with *Rolling Stone* magazine in December 1970, Lennon vented his anger. He denounced the Beatles legacy, claiming he didn't care for most of the Beatles' albums, and said that he'd sold out his original rock and roll ideals for success with the group. He offered tentative praise for the recent solo albums by Harrison and Starr, although he said their music wasn't really to his tastes, but blasted McCartney's solo work. He also attacked those who wouldn't accept his relationship with Ono. He even criticized Bob Dylan for changing his name. "Zimmerman is his name," he pointed out, referring to

Dylan's birth name. "My name isn't John Beatle, it's John Lennon. Just like that."

Lennon's primal therapy ended after four months, when his U. S. visa expired. Back in England, his anger subsided somewhat, and he surprised everyone by adopting a softer rhetorical tone in the 1971 album, *Imagine*. Its title song was inspired by a 1964 book by Ono called *Grapefruit* that was full of short passages often beginning with, "Imagine . . .". Lennon asked listeners to imagine a world with no quarreling religions, nations, or greed, where people lived in peace.

"Imagine" was criticized in several quarters. Theologians and religious conservatives objected to the song's promotion of a world without religion and other critics remarked on Lennon's immense wealth with the line, "Imagine John Lennon with no possessions." Overall response, though, was overwhelmingly positive. Both the *Imagine* album and its title song hit number one in the U.S. and British markets. Lennon observed that, "because it is sugar coated, it is accepted. Now I understand what you have to do. Put your political message across with a little honey."

The rest of the album was largely inspired by Lennon's new autobiographical approach, though it was not as angry as *John Lennon/Plastic Ono Band*. There were love songs for Ono, such as "Oh My Love" and "Ok Yoko," while "How Do You Sleep?" was a criticism of McCartney, who had allegedly criticized the Ono-Lennons in some of his new songs. "Jealous Guy" and "Crippled Inside" were admissions that Lennon had caused others pain because of his own insecurity.

"Imagine" was accompanied by a film of Lennon performing the song on a white grand piano, in a solid white room in his English mansion. One by one, Ono opened large windows around him. It was widely shown on television, and is today considered to be one of the first successful music videos.

Soon after releasing the album, the Ono-Lennons returned to the U.S. to try to retrieve Ono's daughter Kyoko Cox, who lived there with her father. The attempt failed, but the couple decided they liked New York and wanted to live there. "It's like the Rome of today, a bit like a together Liverpool," Lennon said. "I'd always like to be where the action is . . . The seventies are gonna be America's."

Lennon on his white grand piano in his home in England. (Courtesy of Tom Hanley/Redferns)

Almost immediately after settling in New York they were courted by Abbie Hoffman and Jerry Rubin, part of the "Chicago Seven" group of left-wing radicals who were accused of violently disrupting the 1968 U.S. Democratic National Convention. "I'd just arrived in New York," Lennon explained, "and all these people, Jerry Rubin, Abbie Hoffman, David Peel, they were right on the corner when I was going out for a walk in the [Greenwich] Village. It was that kind of community. I loved it. As usual, Lennon falls in the deep end, goes overboard, no half measures. At the time, though, it was a good scene and they meant no harm."

In December 1971, Lennon performed at a rally organized to free John Sinclair, the leader of the White Panther Party, a radical Detroit-based activist group that advocated an overthrow of the government. Sinclair had been arrested for passing two marijuana joints to an undercover policewoman and given an unusually harsh sentence of ten years in prison. The Ono-Lennons joined a bill that included Stevie Wonder, Bob Seger, Phil Ochs, and the White Panther affiliated rock group the MC5, to perform for a crowd of fifteen thousand in Ann Arbor, Michigan. The Ono-Lennons didn't take the stage until three in the morning and only performed four new songs on acoustic guitars, but the attention they drew to the event helped Sinclair receive a pardon within three days. Soon, radicals and activists began seeking out Lennon's support for their causes.

President Richard Nixon paid close attention to Lennon. Nixon and his advisors were afraid radicals were going to disrupt the Republican National Convention in 1972, just as they had the Democratic Party's Convention in 1968. There was even a rumor circulating that Lennon would throw his prestige and fund-raising potential behind such an effort.

U.S. authorities refused to renew the Ono-Lennons' visa after their four months expired in 1972, again using Lennon's British drug conviction as a justification. They said he was a dangerous alien. New York Mayor John Lindsay appealed to the federal government on the couple's behalf, maintaining that the real reason for the deportation was that they, "speak out with strong and critical voices on the major issues of the day." As was later revealed, Lindsay was right. President Richard Nixon and his advisors feared the influence the charismatic and popular Lennon, a frequent critic of Nixon and the Vietnam War, might have over America's youth.

Several weeks before Lennon's visa renewal was denied, South Carolina Republican Senator Strom Thurmond sent a secret memo to the attorney general claiming that Lennon planned to participate in a concert tour that would mix political messages, such as urging people to vote against Nixon, with music. Thurmond recommended that Lennon be deported.

J. Edgar Hoover, the head of the FBI, started working against Lennon as well. He ordered that Lennon be followed and for his phone to be wire tapped. This was a common strategy Hoover used against hundreds of people whose politics he disagreed with. Hoover also began leaking unverifiable rumors to the press implying Lennon was actively supporting violence against the government.

Lennon's attorney, Leon Wilde, received a temporary visa extension after uncovering cases of 118 illiegal immigrants who were allowed resident status despite having been convicted of crimes such as murder, rape, burglary, and more serious drug offenses than Lennon's. "Murders, rapists, multiple convictions for dope, heroin, cocaine. What the hell. I'll fit right in," Lennon remarked.

In the summer of 1972, with his immigration status temporarily in the hands of his lawyers and the court, Lennon followed up his hugely successful *Imagine* with a double album of new politically charged songs called *Some Time In New York City*. The album sold poorly. Meanwhile, Lennon and Ono spent the summer traveling around California, tracking Ono's daughter, Kyoko, who was living there with her father. During this period, Lennon grew apart from his radical friends, and focused on getting over a methadone addiction. He resurfaced for a concert at Madison Square Garden, in New York City, at the end of August. Lennon and Ono headlined the event, a benefit for a hospital for mentally handicapped children. This concert was recorded as *John Lennon- Live In New York City*.

In November of 1972, Nixon was reelected president, to the chagrin of Lennon. On election night, Lennon and Ono attended a party thrown by Rubin. While the crowd watched the results of the election on television, Lennon got drunk and angry. He began to rant and rave and late in the evening disappeared into a bedroom with a woman.

When he emerged sometime later, it was no secret that he had loudly cheated on his wife, while she waited just a room away.

However hurt Ono may have been, she wasn't ready to part from her husband. They decided to move from New York's Greenwich Village to a one-hundred-year-old luxury apartment building called the Dakota, in Manhattan's Upper West Side. Lennon theorized, "Success is something I can take or leave. But I suppose you have to take it before you can decide to leave it." Lennon also shifted his emphasis from extremist politics to appearances at a concert raising money to fight mental retardation, and at comedian Jerry Lewis' Muscular Dystrophy Telethon.

In 1973, Lennon returned to his introspective side in the album *Mind Games*. The title track is named for another self-help book of consciousness-raising exercises that Lennon had discovered, and as usual, had thrown himself into. Though thematically similar to *Imagine*, the album was neither a critical or commercial success. It seemed to many that Lennon's mind was not focused on music.

In October 1973, the source of his distraction became clear. JohnandYoko, who had rarely been apart for more than a day for the past five years, announced they were separating.

eight

Better and Better

After he became a public figure, Lennon was often torn between a desire to shock the world, and the desire to be embraced by it. He explained:

> I always was a rebel because of whatever sociological thing gave me a chip on my shoulder. But on the other hand, I want to be loved and accepted. That's why I'm on stage, like a performing flea. It's because I would like to belong. A part of me would like to be accepted by all facets of society and not be this loudmouth, lunatic poet/musician. But I cannot be what I'm not. What the hell do you do?

In 1973, as he struggled to come to terms with these opposite impulses, Lennon was also embroiled in legal battles over his U.S. immigration status and the division of assets amassed by the Beatles and the ill-fated Apple enterprise. He hadn't released a hit record since *Imagine*, three years earlier. On top of this, his relationship with Ono had come apart. "Yoko and I had a breakdown, one way or another," he reflected. "We were together just about

Lennon with May Pang, who worked as his and Yoko's assistant when she became involved in a love affair with Lennon. (Courtesy of Michael Ochs Archives)

twenty-four hours of every day! So it was bound to happen that we'd snap."

The exact details of the breakup are unclear, though a common element in all versions of the story that became public is Ono and Lennon's assistant, May Pang.

Lennon had earler begun an affair with Pang, who'd been hired in 1971. The twenty-three-year-old Pang accompanied Lennon to Los Angeles. Ono later maintained that she kicked Lennon out of the house and told Pang to look after him. Elliot Mintz, a friend and employee of the Ono-Lennons, said, "Yoko knew it was likely there would be intimacy between the two of them. She took a more mature view, knowing John: 'Better with May than galloping around with the golden groupies.'"

Pang later claimed Ono had walked into Pang's office at the Dakota and announced that she and Lennon were on the verge of separation, and that he would probably start seeing other women. "I know he likes you," Ono said. "If he should ask you to go out with him, you should go."

Ono's pushing of Pang and Lennon together probably came from Ono's fear that Lennon would not be able to take care of himself. For most of his life, he had been looked after by others—first by Aunt Mimi, then by Cynthia, Ono, and a team of assistants. Pang became his lover, but also tried to provide him emotional support because Lennon had always relied on close relationships and partnerships to ground him emotionally.

In late 1973 Lennon and Pang moved to Los Angeles, which Lennon later called, "The City of a Million Nuts . . . In this city everybody's up all night with no place to go." Their first stop was a bank. Remarkably, Lennon had never done much banking before. Amused by the novelty of handling his own money for the first time in more than ten years, he amassed $10,000 by cashing one hundred $100 traveler's checks. "It felt exactly the same as anywhere," he said. "All I did was autograph bits of paper."

Though the Ono-Lennons were separated, Ono called Lennon every morning and night. Pang said:

> Yoko, indeed, had no intention of leaving us alone. She had once
> told me about the Japanese puppet theater. Unlike an American
> puppet show, the Japanese puppet masters were in full view of
> the audience, and the puppets didn't have strings. Even though
> I was three thousand miles away from Yoko, suddenly I felt part
> of one of those shows.

In Los Angeles, Lennon began heavily drinking. When drunk, he wasn't concerned about the impression he made on people. After a concert by one of his childhood idols, Jerry Lee Lewis, Lennon sank to the floor and kissed Lewis's feet. "That's all right, son," Lewis said. "You just get up now."

Lennon went to Las Vegas one weekend and lost a fortune at a casino using his "John Lennon Las Vegas System" that consisted of laying a ten-dollar chip on every number of the roulette table.

One evening, Lennon went to see the Smothers Brothers comedy duo with Pang and musician Harry Nilsson, a frequent drinking companion. Lennon and Nilsson were drunk by the time the Smothers Brothers took the stage, and they proceeded to heckle the comedians and to sing loudly. Lennon got into a fight and was thrown out, but not before passionately kissing Pang in front of photographers. A few days later, a photo of their kiss was published in *Time* magazine with an article that began, "John Lennon has separated from his wife Yoko Ono, and is living it up in L.A."

Lennon wanted to record an album of his favorite 1950s rock songs. It seemed like a good way for him to rediscover his love of music, and reconnect with fans that might have been turned off by his more recent efforts. He recruited Phil Spector to produce it. Spector was a legend for producing many hits of the early 1960s, such as the Ronette's "Be My Baby," which featured his trademark "Wall of Sound" production style that later inspired Brian Wilson in his creation of *Pet Sounds*, which in turn prompted *Sgt. Pepper*. Spector had helped prepare *Let It Be* for release, and had also produced several of Lennon's solo albums, including *Imagine*.

Although the studio was full of some of the greatest minds in popular music, the recording of the album was a fiasco. Spector was a notorious and eccentric perfectionist who demanded the musicians record their parts over and over. Lennon often wouldn't begin to record his vocal parts until two or three in the morning. With little to do in the studio while they waited for their turn to record, Lennon and the other musicians began drinking and using drugs. "I was overwhelmed by the ugliness of the sessions," Pang marveled. "I had never before experienced such self-indulgence and basic disrespect for human values." One night, Lennon got so drunk Spector and a bodyguard tied him to his bed for his own safety.

Spector was known for carrying a gun with him. He terrified everyone by firing his pistol into the ceiling at the end of the sessions. He would then seize the tapes and disappear with them into his castlelike mansion. After several months of wrangling with Spector to get the tapes back, only four of the tracks were suitable for an album. A year later, Lennon went in the studio without Spector and

May Pang convinced John to reconnect with his son Julian. (Courtesy of John Rodgers/Redferns)

recorded several more covers. He then compiled cuts from both sessions for an album entitled *Rock 'n' Roll* that was released in 1975.

In April of 1974, Lennon and Pang moved back to New York. He began preparing an album of new material called *Walls and Bridges* that would reveal what a contradictory artist and person Lennon was at the time. "Musically, my mind was just a clutter," he later said. "It was apparent on *Walls and Bridges*, which was the work of a semisick craftsman. There was no inspiration, and it gave an aura of misery."

Lennon also reconnected with his son Julian during his time on the west coast and invited him to visit during the recording of *Walls and Bridges.* Julian accompanied him to the studio on several occasions, and appears on some tracks, once playing the snare drum on "Ya-Ya."

The album's single was recorded with help from Lennon's friend, British pop star Elton John. Called "Whatever Gets You Through the Night," the song detailed time spent drinking and cavorting in L.A. Elton John made Lennon jokingly promise that if the song reached number one on the charts, Lennon would join Elton John on stage.

To Lennon's surprise—his solo work, though successful, didn't always hit number one—"Whatever Gets You Through the Night" climbed to the top of the U.S. charts. On Thanksgiving Day, 1974, Lennon joined Elton John onstage at a concert in New York attended by about twenty thousand people. They played "Whatever Gets You Through The Night," then "Lucy in the Sky with Diamonds," and "I Saw Her Standing There," which Lennon cheerfully announced was a McCartney song. He then left the stage "because it was Elton's show."

Yoko Ono was in the audience and before the show she sent a white gardenia to Lennon's dressing room. Lennon said to Elton John: "Look what Yoko sent me. I'm glad she's not here tonight. I'd never be able to go on."

After his performance, he was shocked to discover Ono waiting for him backstage. It was their first time together in more than a year but it was becoming clear the couple, who'd spoken on the phone almost daily over the previous weeks, wanted to get back together. "It's all right wondering whether the grass is greener on the other

Lennon shared the stage with British musician Elton John during a 1974 Thanksgiving concert in New York. (Courtesy of Steve Morley/Redferns)

side," Lennon said, "but once you get there all you find is more grass."

Lennon and Ono reunited within two months. "I feel like I've been on Sinbad's voyage, you know, and I've battled all those monsters and I've got back," Lennon said. Pang, left alone after Lennon and Ono's reconciliation, later claimed she and Lennon continued to have clandestine meetings for the next few years.

The Ono-Lennons announced in a press release that they were starting over. Lennon told a journalist: "I don't want to grow up, but I'm sick of *not* growing up—that way," he confessed. "There's a better way of doing it . . . (but) I have this fear of the 'normal' thing . . . the ones that settled for the 'deal.' That's what I'm trying to avoid. But I'm sick of trying to avoid it with violence."

With his usual enthusiasm for new challenges, Lennon plunged headlong into his new, normal life with Ono. They decided to have a baby, but it was difficult. She had already suffered three miscarriages, and at forty-two was approaching an age when pregnancy could be more difficult. They consulted an acupuncturist who instructed them to use no alcohol or drugs, except cigarettes for Lennon, and maintain a healthy diet.

It worked, and the Ono-Lennons were soon expecting. He went out and bought baby clothes from a store called Lady Madonna, named after a Beatles hit. "Another bloody McCartney song," Lennon said.

The legal wrangling over the Beatles' finances and legacy was finally drawing to a close. It allowed Lennon and the others to slowly forget the bitterness that had driven them apart, and to remember instead the good times they'd shared. Furthermore, in October, two days before his thirty-fifth birthday, the New York Supreme Court ordered the U.S. Immigration Service to reconsider Lennon's request for resident status. Nixon, meanwhile, had been forced to resign as U.S. president in disgrace over his part in the Watergate Scandal. Ironically, the scandal involved attempts to wiretap Nixon's political opponents, just as they had done to Lennon's phone.

Lennon soon received his Green Card, granting him

permanent resident status, and was informed that he could apply for U.S. citizenship in 1981.

On Lennon's birthday, October 9, Ono delivered an eight-pound, ten-ounce boy they named Sean. Some suggested that Ono timed Sean's birth; he was delivered by caesarian section, to coincide with Lennon's birthday. Regardless, the delivery was fraught with complications. Ono went into convulsions and almost died after receiving the wrong blood type during a transfusion. When her doctor met Lennon, he said, "I've always wanted to meet you, Mr. Lennon. I always enjoyed your music." Lennon responded, "My wife's dying and you wanna talk about *music!*"

Ono recovered and they were soon back home with their son. Lennon began calling Ono "Mother" but she did not spend much of her time looking after the baby. Instead, she managed the Ono-Lennons' financial assets and Lennon became a househusband, devoting his energy to caring for Sean.

Lennon, who had missed most of Julian's childhood, had to struggle to get used to being tied down at home with a baby. "Walking away is much harder than carrying on," he said. "Shouldn't I be, like, going to the office or *something?* Producing *something?* Because I don't exist if my name isn't in the papers or if I don't have a record out or on the charts or whatever."

Eventually, Lennon began to find a sense of purpose in raising his son. "He didn't come out of my belly, but, by God, I made his bones," he said, "because I've attended to every meal, and to how he sleeps, and to the

Lennon and the FBI

In 1981, Jon Wiener, a history professor at the University of California at Irvine, decided to write a book about John Lennon's immigration fight. He filed a request with the FBI asking to see any documents they had about the deportation proceedings against Lennon. The FBI responded that although they had nearly three hundred documents they would not release them for national security reasons.

Wiener was determined to see the files, which he argued was his right under the Freedom of Information Act. He filed a lawsuit in 1983. In a struggle that lasted nearly fifteen years, the FBI maintained its refusal to release the files. Finally, in 1997, the FBI released most of the files. However, they continued to withhold ten documents, claiming they had been given to the U.S. by a foreign power with an agreement that they be kept confidential.

Wiener wondered why the FBI was so keen to keep documents secret about a dead rock star and filed another suit. In 2004 a judge ruled the FBI had to release the final ten documents but the FBI, appealed.

Wiener thinks the hidden documents detail Lennon's involvement with leftist political groups in England between 1969 and 1970. However, because the FBI won't even reveal what country the documents are from, Wiener is unable to verify this.

From studying the released documents, Weiner confirmed that few of them are devoted to Lennon's arrest for drug possession, the ostensible reason for his denial of a U. S. visa. Instead, they focus on his criticism of Nixon and the Vietnam War, his activism and friendship with antiwar protesters Abbie Hoffman and Jerry Rubin, his performance at the John Sinclair rally, which was recorded word for word, and his plan to hold a concert tour during which he would encourage young people to register to vote.

Wiener published his findings in 2000 in the book *Gimme Some Truth: The John Lennon FBI Files.* In 2006, he served as a historical consultant on the film *The U. S. vs. John Lennon*, a documentary detailing Lennon's struggles with the Nixon Administration.

fact that he swims like a fish. That's because I took him to the 'Y.'"

Lennon had help caring for Sean. There was a nanny, a cook, housekeeper, and personal assistant. He had plenty of free time to indulge himself and experiment with different arts. He drew sketches for his son, and had a photographer shoot each of the first 365 days of Sean's life. He baked bread for the first time, and proudly took a picture of his first loaf. Soon, Lennon's bread was being eaten by his staff and friends as soon as it emerged from the oven. "I'd make two loaves on Friday and they'd be gone by Saturday afternoon," he said. "The thrill was wearing off and became routine again."

He had published two short books of prose pieces in the past. Now he started writing again, creating dozens of pages of mad stuff, some with captioned drawings such as: "Every day in every way/I'm getting better & better."

Lennon also reconnected with friends and family he'd lost contact with over the years. Some of the reconnecting had begun during his time in Los Angeles, but his new lifestyle gave him time to continue. He spoke frequently to Aunt Mimi over the phone, and continued trying to rebuild his relationship with Julian.

Lennon also reconciled somewhat with his former bandmates. Even McCartney began visiting Lennon in New York, and while they didn't resume writing music, they did happily reminisce. They also watched TV, talked about their kids, and generally hung out together again.

Ono, meanwhile, focused on overseeing their finances. "When John and I decided that I would be a business-woman," she explained, "I told myself that in order to attract money and do the new job well, I'd have to recon-struct my psyche. My old attitude of not wanting to get into money just wasn't going to do."

Ono learned fast. She bought additional units at their Dakota building, and organic dairy farms in Vermont and Virginia. She even sold a prize Holstein cow for a world record $265,000 at the New York State Fair. "Only Yoko Ono could sell a cow for a quarter of a million dollars," Lennon said.

For advice on matters ranging from business decisions to security, Ono relied on astrologers, tarot card readers, numbers interpreters, and even a directional man who decreed each day whether she and Lennon should travel north, south, east or west. More than once, Lennon was instructed to journey home all the way around the world from a destination instead of taking the most direct route. "Go with it," Lennon once told an assistant. "Trust her. She's always right."

Lennon also mellowed in regard to his musical legacy. His perception of the Beatles years began to change from one of scorn to a more measured appreciation. "I'm always proud and pleased when people do my songs," he said. "It gives me pleasure that they even attempt to do them, because a lot of my songs aren't that doable. I go to restaurants and the groups always play 'Yesterday.' Yoko and I even signed a guy's violin in Spain after he played us 'Yesterday.' He couldn't understand that I didn't write the song. But I guess he couldn't have gone from table to table playing 'I Am The Walrus.'"

He remained adamant, however, that the Beatles were finished for good, though he had collaborated with Starr on the drummer's solo albums. "Talking about the Beatles getting back together is an illusion," he insisted. "That was ten years ago. The Beatles only exist on film and on record and in people's minds. You cannot get back together what no longer exists. We are not those four people anymore."

Lennon began to seem more content and happy. The turmoil and restlessness that had defined his life previously began to seem like a thing of the past, at least temporarily. In 1979, the Ono-Lennons took out full-page ads in New York, London, and Tokyo newspaper entitled a "Love Letter From John and Yoko." It read: "The house is getting very comfortable now. Sean is beautiful. The plants are growing. The cats are purring. The town is shining, sun, rain or snow. We live in a beautiful universe. We are thankful every day for the plentifulness of our life . . . our silence is a silence of love and not of indifference."

Lennon was working on new songs, but at a different pace than before. He was inspired by the new musical movement called punk and its less abrasive offshoot, new wave. He heard this new style at a club in June 1980, and the music's energy and anger appealed to the always-rebellious Lennon. After five years, the Ono-Lennons prepared to make a new record, and, hopefully, be embraced by the world once again.

nine

Dakota Groupies

In August of 1980, after recruiting a group of top studio musicians, John Lennon began recording a new album in New York. He had recently returned from a vacation with Sean in Bermuda and wanted to work with people he had not played with before, instead of celebrity friends like Starr, Elton John, or Eric Clapton. "I was too tight with . . . all the others to get on their backs and say, 'No, I don't like it,'" he explained. "Now I can come in from day one and be the boss."

Drugs and alcohol were not allowed in the studio. Musicians were given snacks of juice, raisins, sunflower seeds, and sushi, which Lennon referred to as dead fish. He also made it clear that he was there to get a job done. One musician described Lennon's approach as:

Look, here's a song. It's real simple. You guys know how to play your instruments. Forget about all the frills. Just accompany me.' You knew that in twenty minutes he was going to start taking the thing and in an hour he wanted it done. It changed your whole approach to the recording because you knew you didn't have three hours to fuss around . . . It made you go for a gut performance.

Lennon had written about two-dozen new songs, and Ono had written several more. The new album was to be called *Double Fantasy*, the name of an orchid Lennon had seen while on vacation. He was determined to make an album that reflected his current life with Ono and Sean.

The album opened with the sound of Ono cheerfully playing a Japanese wishing bell. He sang the first song, "(Just Like) Starting Over," which frankly acknowledged his roots, in a 1950s-style voice, almost an Elvis impersonation. "In the Beatle days, that would have been taken as a joke. One avoided clichés," he said. "But now those clichés aren't clichés any more"

"Beautiful Boy" was written to Sean. Lennon said, "I kept thinking, 'Well, I ought to be able to write about Sean.' I was going through a bit of that and when I finally gave up on thinking about writing a song about him, of course, the song came to me." The song featured the lyric, "Life is what happens to you while you're busy making other plans." Lennon also included the phrase he'd written a year earlier: "Every day, in every way, it's getting better and better."

In "Woman" Lennon acknowledged his mistreatment of women in the past.

*Woman, I can hardly express, my mixed emotions at
my thoughtlessness
After all, I'm forever in your debt
And woman, I will try to express, my inner feelings
and thankfulness,
For showing me the meaning of success.*

"I was the real pig," Lennon confessed. "And it is a relief not to be a pig. The pressures of being a pig were enormous . . . All those years of trying to be tough and the heavy rocker and heavy womanizer and heavy drinker were killing me. And it is a relief not to have to do it."

"Watching the Wheels" was a response to everyone who wondered why the prolific writer was taking so much time between albums. "Pop stars were getting indignant in the press that I wasn't making records," Lennon said. "I couldn't believe it, they were acting like mothers-in-law."

*Lennon wrote the song "Beautiful Boy"
with his son Sean in mind.* (Courtesy
of Pacific Press Service)

*Well they shake their heads and look at me as if I've
lost my mind*
*I tell them there's no hurry I'm just sitting here doing
time*

Lennon produced a number of Ono's songs that bore the
influence of the currently popular new wave groups, like
the B-52's and Blondie. Her song "I'm Your Angel" was
well liked, though the tune was so similar to a hit from
fifty years earlier, "Makin' Whoopee," that Ono was sued
for copyright infringement.

Double Fantasy was eagerly anticipated, and expectations for it had grown to unrealistic levels. When it was
released, Britain's *Melody Maker* complained that "The
whole thing positively reeks of an indulgent sterility. It's
a godawful yawn!" Some fans complained that it was
only half an album because they considered Ono's songs
superfluous. Lennon cared little about their complaints. "We
have resurrected ourselves as John and Yoko," he said. "If
they didn't want the two of us, we weren't interested."

Despite the criticisms, *Double Fantasy* was a big seller
and it shoved the previously withdrawn Ono-Lennons back
into the limelight. They had gone to great lengths to protect their privacy, usually traveling under assumed names,
such as Reverend Fred and Ada Ghurkin. The fake names
fooled few people, but they took other precautions. When
flying, they not only bought first-class airline seats, but
also the entire row in front, back and across from them
to help maintain their privacy and personal space. They

sent and received important documents using their own messengers, because any envelope labeled John Lennon was likely to get ripped open.

They also invested in security. Jack MacDougall, a former FBI agent, was hired to protect them. During the recording of the album, he was alarmed by an article in a New York newspaper that detailed Lennon and Ono's studio location and schedule, even mentioning their route to and from the Dakota. He warned that the article was, "an open invitation for every wacko in the country to come after them." MacDougall recommended that an armed guard accompany them to the studio, but the nonviolent Ono-Lennons refused.

Lennon was more at ease in New York than he had been in London or Los Angeles. He believed that longtime fans had matured with him, and that even new admirers that had grown up in the 1970s lacked the intensity of the previous decade's fans. He was still confronted with the occasional, "When are you going back with the Beatles?" which he often answered with, "When are you going back to high school?" For the most part, though, his attitude toward outsiders and fans had grown more positive, along with his whole outlook on life.

"I'm going to be forty," he said just before his October 1980 birthday, "and life begins at forty, so they promise. Oh, I *believe* it too. Because I feel fine. I'm like, *excited*. It's like twenty-one, you know, hitting twenty-one. It's like: *Wow!* What's going to happen next?"

Though his age had calmed some of his anger, Lennon still was an advocate for social change. He said that his age did not diminish his desire for world peace, and frustration at the violence around him. "Mahatma Gandhi and Martin Luther King are great examples of fantastic nonviolents who died violently," he said. "I can never work that out. We're pacifists, but I'm not sure what it means when you're such a pacifist that you get shot. I can never understand that."

With *Double Fantasy* a success, Lennon went back into the studio to record a follow-up. The press was looking favorably at him for first time in years. It looked as though he was on the way to regaining the worldwide adulation he'd received as a Beatle. But among the millions with a renewed interest in John Lennon was a twenty-five-year-old security guard named Mark David Chapman, from Hawaii. A rabid Beatles fan, he had once worn wireless glasses like Lennon and had played in a rock band that covered many of his songs. But in the intervening years, Chapman had become a born again Christian, and he had a history of mental illness.

In December Chapman flew from Hawaii to New York and began hanging around the Dakota. Chapman got to know other Dakota groupies who waited each day for a glimpse of the Ono-Lennons as well as the other celebrities living in the building, including singer/songwriter Paul Simon, dancer Rudolf Nureyev and composer Leonard Bernstein. He even met and dined with Sean's babysitter.

About five p.m. on Monday, December 8, Lennon and Ono left the Dakota for a recording session. Chapman approached Lennon, and took out a copy of *Double Fantasy,* which Lennon signed before climbing into a waiting limousine. Chapman was especially happy that an amateur photographer had taken a picture of him meeting Lennon. "They'll never believe this in Hawaii," he said.

Just before eleven p.m. that night, Lennon and Ono returned to the Dakota. Lennon was absorbed in listening to tapes of the evening's sessions as they entered the large archway in front of the Dakota. Then Lennon heard someone call him. It was Chapman, crouched in a military stance and pointing a gun.

Before Lennon could turn, Chapman fired two shots into his back, and two more into his shoulder. Lennon staggered up six steps to the back of the Dakota's entrance, moaning "I'm shot!" before falling and shattering his glasses. Ono screamed for help as Chapman dropped his gun. A doorman quickly kicked it out of reach, saying, "Do you know what you just did?"

"I just shot John Lennon," Chapman responded.

Frantic calls brought the first policemen to the scene within two minutes. They apprehended Chapman as he read a copy of his favorite book *The Catcher in the Rye*, by J.D. Salinger. He was also carrying a Bible and fourteen hours of Beatles tapes. Another squad car rushed Lennon to a hospital. But it was too late; Lennon died from a massive loss of blood.

Chapman was quickly transferred to a heavily guarded psychiatric ward to prevent someone from killing him in revenge. Over time his motives were revealed. Apparently, Chapman had decided that Lennon, his onetime hero, had become complacent and decadent and was a dangerous influence on young people. Chapman also took offense to "Imagine's" plea to visualize a world without heaven or religion. He had also projected himself into the role of the main character of *Catcher in the Rye,* who harbored a fantasy of being a guardian of young people, catching them before they fell into danger. In short, Chapman had decided that it was his duty to protect the world from John Lennon.

Word of Lennon's murder sped through Manhattan and the world. Within a few hours hundreds of fans had gathered at the Dakota. Millions of Americans first

Fans gather outside the Dakota apartment building shortly after learning of Lennon's murder. (Courtesy of the Associated Press)

learned of Lennon's death when announcer Howard Cosell interrupted his popular *Monday Night Football* broadcast to break the news. "I was devastated," Cosell recalled. "We were in the midst of a tied football game that was about to go into overtime, and I was wrestling with the problem of breaking the news on TV, thinking that, even in this sick, sports-obsessed country, *this* is more important than any goddamned football game will ever be."

Musician Bruce Springsteen received the news just before a concert and broke it to his audience. "It is a hard night to come out and play when so much has been lost," he said. "The first song I ever learned to play was a record called 'Twist and Shout' and if it wasn't for John Lennon, we'd all be in a different place tonight."

The crowd around the Dakota grew into the thousands, spilling into Central Park across the street. One person passed out sticks of incense; another, bottles of beer. All those gathered were devastated and shocked. Someone began singing "Give Peace a Chance," and soon the entire crowd sang the chorus for more than thirty minutes.

Radio stations had by now received the news, and a steady stream of songs by Lennon and the Beatles were played through the night as Ono secluded herself in the Dakota.

The next day she told Sean, who asked why anyone would want to kill his father. The young boy was oblivious to Lennon's fame. He had only recently seen *Yellow Submarine* on television and asked, "Daddy, were you a Beatle?" When Ono explained that the killer's fate was up to the court, he wondered if she meant a tennis or basketball court. "That's how Sean used to talk with his father," Ono said in a statement. "They were buddies. Lennon would have been proud of Sean if he had heard this. Sean cried later. He also said, 'Now Daddy is part of God. I guess when you die you become much more bigger because you're part of everything.'"

In Liverpool, Aunt Mimi was in bed when she heard the news on the radio. She fell into a state of shock until friends and family started making concerned phone calls. She was later amazed to discover she had unknowingly picked up a scissors and began cutting off her hair. "I will never recover," she said.

McCartney emerged from his home the next day, seemingly traumatized. His first mumbled words, "It's a drag, isn't it?," were interpreted by some as uncaring. Later that day, McCartney secured himself in a studio with George Martin and they spent the afternoon consoling each other. Harrison retreated into his house, refusing calls from anyone for almost a day.

Starr, who lived in New York, had shared Thanksgiving dinner with the Ono-Lennons only two weeks earlier. He rushed back from a vacation to find that so many people surrounded the Dakota that he had to leave his car and pick his way through on foot. Disgusted at people tearing at his clothing and besieging him for autographs, he visited Ono and Sean for a few hours, and then disappeared into seclusion, refusing to speak to the media. Several other musicians, including Mick Jagger, Elton John, Bob Dylan and Eric Clapton were also too stunned to offer immediate reaction. Ray Charles complained that, "it's easier to get a gun in this country than a driver's license."

Ono tried to keep a low profile. She had Lennon's body secretly cremated, and Jack MacDougall, who had earlier warned Ono to hire an armed guard for Lennon, had the task of returning his ashes to the Dakota. When asked at the door the contents of the package he carried, MacDougall replied, "That was the greatest rock musician in the world."

Within two days of Lennon's killing, two Americans committed suicide. Ono responded quickly. "This is not the end of an era," she assured. "'Starting Over' still goes. The Eighties are going to be a beautiful time . . . I wish I could tell you how hard it is . . . But when something like this happens, each one of us must go on."

Ono also directed a comment to people, especially in Britain, who decried New York as a lawless city responsible for Lennon's death: "People say there is something wrong with New York, that it's sick. But John loved New York. He'd be the first to say it wasn't New York's fault. There can be one crank anywhere."

Though Ono had not planned a formal funeral for Lennon, she realized the need for millions of fans throughout the world to say goodbye. She asked for well-wishers, wherever they were, to remember him with ten minutes of silent prayer on Sunday, December 14, at 2 p.m. New York time.

In Liverpool that day, a crowd of more than 30,000 gathered around a church, and fell silent at the appointed time. Vigils were held in dozens of other communities, the largest in Manhattan's Central Park. Ono did not attend, but could see from her home at the Dakota about 100,000 people gathered in the park to remember Lennon. His songs played over loudspeakers, and the crowd sang along and flashed peace signs.

At 2 p.m., the crowd went silent, and all radios were turned off. At the end of the prayer vigil, "Imagine" was played over the loudspeakers. As the crowd dispersed, snow began to fall.

Even more people began buying Lennon albums, especially *Double Fantasy*, his last work. The single "Starting Over," which was number four at the time of Lennon's death, went to number one for five weeks, and the album soon topped the charts. *Double Fantasy* received the Grammy Award for 1981 Album of the Year. "Imagine," re-released after ten years, climbed to the top of the charts for a second time.

Many other musicians released tributes to Lennon. Harrison wrote "All Those Years Ago," which eulogized Lennon with lines such as:

You said it all though not many had ears, all those years ago
You had control of our smiles and our tears, all those years ago

The song included accompaniment by McCartney and Starr, marking their first time together on record since the Beatles broke up. McCartney wrote his own song, "Here Today," which said, "I still remember how it was before, and I am holding back the tears no more." Elton John, Billy Joel, Paul Simon, Jackson Browne, Pink Floyd and Queen all released tributes.

In 1984, Ono released the rest of Lennon's songs from the session that yielded *Double Fantasy,* along with her own in an album entitled *Milk and Honey.* In addition to releasing a number of albums, including one in 2001, and pursuing a number of different art projects, she devoted much of her energy to looking after Lennon's legacy.

Lennon's death was especially difficult for his son, Julian. Shortly before his death, Lennon had offhandedly made a remark in a major magazine interview that Julian was accidentally "born out of a bottle of whiskey on a Saturday night." He had also said that though he loved both his sons, "Sean is a planned child, and therein lies the difference."

To Julian, by then a teenager, the remark deepened wounds he already felt from being abandoned. "The person that had to deal with the actual real-life person . . .who was always away and who, for many years, didn't remain in touch with me and didn't seem to care."

Julian Lennon later became a singer/songwriter. His debut album *Valotte,* received a Grammy nomination for Best New Artist of 1986. Though Julian wasn't trying to mimic his father, his voice and even appearance were similar to John Lennon's. He has since released several moderately successful albums.

Sean Lennon also embarked on a musical career in the 1990s. He toured with alternative band Cibo Matto as a bassist, and in 1998 released a critically applauded album called *Into The Sun*. In 2006, he released its follow up, *Friendly Fire*.

Over the years, many fans hoped that there might be a Beatles reunion, with Julian filling in for his father. This never came to pass though, and the notion was forgotten after the death of George Harrison from cancer in 2001.

The Beatles did reunite in the studio in the 1990s. Referred to as the Threetles, McCartney, Harrison, and Starr added their harmonies and accompaniment to two taped songs Lennon had recorded alone at his home. One of the songs, "Free As A Bird" was released as a single and climbed to number six on the charts in 1996.

The Beatles remain the top-selling band in history, with almost 169 million albums sold. As of 2005, Lennon, McCartney, Harrison and Starr—together or alone—have scored at least one album in the U.S. or British top ten *every* year since 1962. Lennon sold fourteen million solo albums after the Beatles' breakup.

When the BBC conducted a national vote to determine the "100 Greatest Britons," Lennon placed eighth. He was joined in the top ten by notable individuals such as William Shakespeare, Queen Elizabeth I, Isaac Newton, Charles Darwin, and Winston Churchill.

"He was brilliant, he was happy, he was angry, he was sad," Ono once said. "Above all, he was a genius who worked hard to give his best to the world. It was nice to know that such a person was part of our generation, our century, and the human race."

timeline

1940   John Winston Lennon is born October 9,
in Liverpool, England.

1946   Chooses to live with his mother rather than his
father; is given to his Aunt Mimi.

1957   Buys guitar and forms the Quarry Men; meets
Paul McCartney, who joins band; enters
Liverpool Art College, meets Stuart
Sutcliffe, Cynthia Powell.

1958   Mother killed; George Harrison joins the
Quarry Men.

1959   Sutcliffe and drummer Pete Best join
Quarry Men.

1960   Quarry Men change name to the Beatles,
plays several months of nightly gigs in
Hamburg, Germany.

1961 Back in Liverpool, the Beatles become popular attraction at the Cavern Club.

1962 Brian Epstein becomes Beatles' manager; Pete Best is fired and replaced with Ringo Starr; Sutcliffe dies from a brain hemorrhage; Lennon marries Cynthia; the Beatles cut their first album and their single, "Love Me Do," enters the charts.

1963 The Beatles top British singles and album charts; son Julian is born.

1964 73 million people watch the Beatles on *The Ed Sullivan Show*; in one week of April the Beatles hold the top five U.S. singles spots and top two album positions; Beatles film *A Hard Day's Night* is shot and released; Father makes contact.

1965 Beatles play for 55,000 fans in New York; band releases film, *Help,* and album, *Rubber Soul.*

1966 Beatles release *Revolver*; band quits touring.

1967 Beatles release *Sgt. Pepper's Lonely Heart's Club Band;* open Apple Boutique; release film and album *Magical Mystery Tour.*

1968 Beatles travel to India to meditate with the Maharishi; Lennon divorces Cynthia, begins affair with Yoko Ono; Ono suffers a miscarriage; Beatles' *White Album* is released.

1969 The Beatles record *Abbey Road*; Lennon and Ono marry and conduct "Bed-Ins" for peace and "bag happenings"; with the Plastic Ono Band records first solo single, "Give Peace a Chance."

1970 Beatles officially split up; records *John Lennon/Plastic Ono Band* album.

1971 Releases *Imagine;* title song becomes his best-selling post-Beatles single; comes to the U.S; is quickly recruited for American radical political causes.

1972 Visa is not renewed, battles to remain in America; shifts benefit concert appearances from left-wing politics to charities such as the Jerry Lewis Muscular Dystrophy Telethon.

1973 Separates from Ono and moves to Los Angeles with May Pang.

1974 Releases *Walls and Bridges;* single "Whatever Gets You Through the Night" goes to No. 1.

1975 Reunites with Yoko; son Sean is born.

1976 Receives Green Card as permanent U.S. resident.

1980 Releases *Double Fantasy;* is murdered by Mark David Chapman; dozens of worldwide candle-light vigils include a gathering of 100,000 in New York's Central Park.

1981 *Double Fantasy* becomes Lennon's best-selling
solo album and yields three top ten singles;
"Imagine" re-released and is a No. 1
single for the second time.

1982 *Double Fantasy* receives Grammy Award as
1981 Album of the Year.

1995 Former Beatles reunite on audio as McCartney,
Harrison, and Starr record their parts over a 1977
demo tape Lennon recorded at home called "Free As
A Bird;" charts at number six, twenty-five years after
the band broke up.

Sources

CHAPTER ONE: War Time

p. 12, "Take this blanket off . . ." Bill Harry, *The John Lennon Encyclopedia,* (London: Virgin Publishing, 2000), 696.

p. 12, "the others are all wrinkled . . ." Ray Coleman, *Lennon, the Definitive Biography,* (New York: Harper Perennial, 1985), 99.

p. 13, "You look silly," Julia Baird, *John Lennon: My Brother*, (New York: Jove Books, 1988), 9.

p. 14, "Mummy, mummy!" Coleman, *Lennon, the Definitive Biography,* 94.

p. 15, "Sometimes when John . . ." Harry, *The John Lennon Encyclopedia*, 819.

p. 16, "sharp as a needle . . ." Coleman, *Lennon, the Definitive Biography,* 103.

p. 16, "His mind was going . . ." James Henke, *Lennon Legend* (San Francisco, Chronicle Books, 2003), 6.

p. 16, "He always had to be in charge . . ." Coleman, *Lennon, the Definitive Biography,* 96.

p. 17, "John, even then . . ." Pete Shotton and Nicholas Schaffner, *John Lennon in My Life*, (Briarcliff Manor, NY: Stein and Day, 1983), 24.

p. 18, "As soon as . . ." Hunter Davies, *The Beatles*, (New York: Dell, 1968), 10.

p. 18-19, "I used to think . . ." Jann Wenner, *Lennon Remembers* (London: Verso, 2000), 36.

p. 19, "A poor result . . ." Copy of John Lennon's 1953 report card.

p. 19, "He is so fond . . ." Copy of John Lennon's 1955 report card.

p. 19, "He is certainly . . ." Copy of John Lennon's 1956 report card.

p. 19, "Yes . . . and no . . ." Undated copy of John's *Daily Howl* newspaper.

p. 19, "Our late editor . . ." Ibid.

p. 19, "I looked at all . . ." Harry, *The John Lennon Encyclopedia*, 737.

p. 20, "they parted and out came . . ." Davies, *The Beatles*, 12.

CHAPTER TWO: Quarry Men

p. 22, "One of them had . . ." Harry, *The John Lennon Encyclopedia*, 313.

p. 23, "Don't ever get . . ." Baird, *John Lennon: My Brother*, 20.

p. 24, "Don't worry about school . . ." Albert Goldman, *The Lives of John Lennon*, (New York: William Morrow, 1988), 54.

p. 25, "Guaranteed not to split . . ." Henke, *Lennon Legend*, 9.

p. 25, "The guitar's all very well . . ." Shotton and Schaffner, *John Lennon in My Life*, 51.

p. 25-26, "He leaned so long . . ." Goldman, *The Lives of John Lennon*, 62.

p. 28, "Before Elvis . . ." Baird, *John Lennon: My Brother*, 42.

p. 28, "He became a mess . . ." Henke, *Lennon Legend*, 9.

p. 28, "I couldn't take my eyes . . ." Coleman, *Lennon, the Definitive Biography*, 145.

p. 29, "By the way . . ." Shotton and Schaffner, *John Lennon in My Life*, 55.

p. 29, "Be careful of . . ." Coleman, *Lennon, the Definitive Biography*, 164.

p. 30, "like a comedy act . . ." Baird, *John Lennon: My Brother*, 49.

p. 31, "Well, that takes care of . . ." Shotton and Schaffner, *John Lennon in My Life*, 58.

p. 31, " I knew that the destruction . . ." Ibid.

p. 31, "You should try to get into . . ." Coleman, *Lennon, the Definitive Biography*, 131.

p. 31-32, "Though I have yet . . ." Shotton and Schaffner, *John Lennon in My Life*, 22.

p. 32, "Don't worry . . ." Coleman, *Lennon, the Definitive Biography,* 169.

p. 32, "I lost her twice . . ." David Sheff, *All We Are Saying*, (New York: St. Martin's Press, 2000), 162.

CHAPTER THREE: Birth of the Beatles

p. 33, "There was a famous . . ." "Beatles History, 1958," http://www.beatles-discography.com/1958.html (Accessed May 23, 2005).

p. 34, "They should've . . ." Shotton and Schaffner, *John Lennon in My Life*, 61.

p. 34, "Even I sometimes . . ." Ibid.

p. 35, "that I had nothing . . ." Goldman, *The Lives of John Lennon*, 80.

p. 35, "a right Holylake runt . . ." Davies, *The Beatles*, 57.

p. 35, "I didn't ask . . ." Goldman, *The Lives of John Lennon*, 82.

p. 35, "I was in sort of . . ." Davies, *The Beatles*, 59.

p. 37, "We wrote a lot . . . " Sheff, *All We Are Saying*, 137.

p. 37, "a beautiful period . . . " Coleman, *Lennon, the Definitive Biography,* 190.

p. 39, "We were making . . ." Davies, *The Beatles*, 75.

p. 40-41, "We had all sorts of . . ." http://www.beatles-discography.com/1960.html (Accessed May 24, 2005)

p. 41, "You could just about . . ." Ibid.

p. 41, "We'd try to . . ." Davies, *The Beatles*, 85.

p. 45, "Postman, postman . . ." Coleman, *Lennon, the Definitive Biography*, 203.

p. 47, "Once his mind was set . . ." Ibid., 218.

p. 47, "It was great . . ." http://www.beatles-discography.com/1957.html (Accessed May 25, 2005)

p. 48, "I was raised . . ." Henke, *Lennon Legend*, 12.

p. 48, "I can't remember . . ." Harry, *The John Lennon Encyclopedia*, 882.

p. 48, "My Bonnie . . ." Davies, *The Beatles*, 144.

p. 49, "I had been bothered . . ." Coleman, *Lennon, the Definitive Biography,* 244.

p. 49, "They smoked as they played . . ." Davies, *The Beatles*, 141.

p. 50, "This is disgraceful . . ." Ibid., 143.

p. 50, "Right, then, Brian . . ." Coleman, *Lennon, the Definitive Biography,* 247.

CHAPTER FOUR: Beatlemania

p. 51, "I'll wear a . . ." http://www.beatles-discography.com/1962.html (Accessed May 28, 2005).

p. 52, "I'd say to George . . ." Coleman, *Lennon, the Definitive Biography*, 249.

p. 53, "He told me . . ." Davies, *The Beatles*, 149.

p. 54, "I thought they were . . ." Henke, Lennon Legend, 15.

p. 54, "Please wire . . ." Coleman, Lennon, the Definitive Biography, 278.

p. 55, "I don't think . . ." Ibid., 263.

p. 56, "Oh Christ . . ." Baird, John Lennon: My Brother, 74.

p. 56, "More like a funeral . . ." Ibid., 75.

p. 57, "We were cowards . . ." Davies, The Beatles, 159.

p. 57, "They're buying . . ." http://www.beatles-discography.com/1962.html (Accessed June 13, 2005).

p. 57, "I told them . . ." Davies, The Beatles, 185.

p. 57, "Gentlemen, you've made . . ." Goldman, The Lives of John Lennon, 131.

p. 58, "I suppose . . ." Davies, *The Beatles*, 194.

p. 59, "Don't let . . ." Coleman, *Lennon, the Definitive Biography*, 281.

p. 59, "He's not the brute . . ." Goldman, *The Lives of John Lennon*, 134.

p. 60, "Walking about married . . ." Shotton and Schaffner, *John Lennon in My Life*, 72.

p. 60, "Who's going to . . ." Baird, *John Lennon: My Brother*, 77.

p. 61, "Will the people . . ." Coleman, *Lennon, the Definitive Biography*, 306.

p. 61-62, "Yeah! Yeah! Yeah! . . ." http://www.beatles discography.com/1963.html (Accessed June 13, 2005).

p. 65, "What do you think . . ." http://www.beatles discography.com/1964.html (Accessed June 13, 2005).

p. 67, "Dear Alf . . ." Goldman, *The Lives of John Lennon*, 288.

p. X, "One stroke . . ." Tom Hoving in discussion with the author, May 2005.

p. 69, "They all stood . . ." Ibid.

p. 69, "I never thought . . ." http://www.beatles discography.com/1963.html (Accessed June 14, 2005).

p. 69, "Would you like . . ." Goldman, *The Lives of John Lennon*, 173.

p. 69-70, "I see you . . ." Coleman, *Lennon, the Definitive Biography*, 296.

p. 70, "I reckon . . ." Henke, *Lennon Legend*, 22.

CHAPTER FIVE: Different Mental Planes

p. 72, "You stick . . ." Harry, *The John Lennon Encyclopedia*, 233.

p. 73, "I feel . . ." Jann Wenner, untitled article, *Rolling Stone*, November 9, 1967, 16.

p. 74, "Christianity will go . . ." Goldman, *The Lives of John Lennon*, 205.

p. 74-75, "I'm not saying . . ." http://www.beatles discography.com/1966.html (Accessed June 16, 2005).

p. 75, "I hate war . . ." Coleman, *Lennon, the Definitive Biography*, 413.

p. 77, "But what about . . ." Harry, *The John Lennon Encyclopedia*, 218.

p. 78, "We were on . . ." Coleman, *Lennon, the Definitive Biography*, 322.

p. 79, "We transformed it . . ." Harry, *The John Lennon Encyclopedia*, 867.

p. 80, "My son came home . . ." http://www.beatles discography.com/l.html (Accessed June 20, 2005).

p. 80, "John wasn't like that . . ." Ibid.

p. 82, "There was nothing . . ." Coleman, *Lennon, the Definitive Biography*, 421.

p. 83, "Look, I don't . . ." Ibid., 419.

p. 83, "Suppose I drive . . ." Goldman, *The Lives of John Lennon*, 244.

p. 84, "Watch all the lights . . ." Coleman, *Lennon, the Definitive Biography*, 426.

p. 85, "Oh, don't worry . . ." Ibid., 429.

p. 85, "I knew . . ." Harry, *The John Lennon Encyclopedia*, 233..

p. 86, "The Magical Mystery Tour . . ." http://www. beatlesdiscography.com/1967.html (Accessed June 21, 2005).

p. 87, "We were all wondering . . ." http://www.beatles discography.com/1968.html (Accessed June 21, 2005).

p. 87, "Every morning . . ." Coleman, *Lennon, the Definitive Biography*, 433.

p. 87, "I'm a cloud . . ." Ibid., 434.

p. 88, "I was going . . ." Goldman, *The Lives of John Lennon*, 294.

p. X, "If you're so . . ." Coleman, *Lennon, the Definitive Biography*, 435.

p. 88, "Actually, Pete, . . ." Shotton and Schaffner, *John Lennon in My Life*, 162.

CHAPTER SIX: Death of the Beatles

p. 89, "It's only money . . ." Shotton and Schaffner, *John Lennon in My Life*, 148.

p. 89, "We could have . . ." Harry, *The John Lennon Encyclopedia*, 30.

p. 90, "The aim of the company . . ." Ibid.

p. 90, "From the business . . ." Shotton and Schaffner, *John Lennon in My Life*, 150.

p. 92-93, "I didn't know . . ." Wenner, *Lennon Remembers*, 40.

p. 93, "I suppose . . ." Coleman, *Lennon, the Definitive Biography,* 438.

p. 94, "Where's your wife . . ." Coleman, *Lennon, the Definitive Biography,* 456.

p. 95, "I felt like a baby . . ." Goldman, *The Lives of John Lennon*, 311.

p. 95, "As soon as . . ." Sheff, *All We Are Saying*, 48.

p. 95, "Hey Jules . . ." Shotton and Schaffner, *John Lennon in My Life*, 179.

p. 97-98, "That was a bit . . ." Harry, *The John Lennon Encyclopedia*, 686.

p. 98, "They insulted her…" Wenner, *Lennon Remembers*, 44.

p. 100, "I'm (now) not . . ." Ibid., 761.

p. 101, "fed up with being . . ." Wenner, *Lennon Remembers*, 23.

p. 101, "I want people . . ." Ibid., 939.

p. 101, "Well, aren't you . . ." Goldman, *The Lives of John Lennon*, 316.

p. 105, "I'm warming to . . ." Ibid., 323.

p. 106, "I'd like to say . . ." Ibid., 326.

p. 110, "The others were animals …" Wenner, *Lennon Remembers*, 122.

p. 112, "Let's get back . . . it had to happen" Coleman, *Lennon, the Definitive Biography,* 472.

p. 113, "Paul hasn't left . . ." Ibid., 480.

CHAPTER SEVEN: JohnandYoko

p. 114, "We are two . . ." Coleman, *Lennon, the Definitive Biography,* 492.

p. 114, "We're going to stage . . ." Jonathan Cott and Christine Doudna, *The Ballad of John and Yoko*, 35.

p. 115, "The press would have . . ." Coleman, *Lennon, the Definitive Biography,* 494.

p. 117, "It is the most . . ." Goldman, *The Lives of John Lennon*, 345.

p. 117-118, "If we, or anybody . . ." http://www.beatles-discography.com/1969.html (Accessed June 30, 2005).

p. 118, "I think that I . . ."w Henke, *Lennon Legend*, 35.

p. 118, "she enabled . . ." Shotton and Schaffner, *John Lennon in My Life*, 171.

p. 118-119, "I can't remember . . ." Cott and Doudna, *The Ballad of John and Yoko*, 37.

p. 120, "showed me how . . ." http://www.beatles discography.com/1970.html (Accessed July 4, 2005).

p. 121-122, "My name isn't . . ." Wenner, *Lennon Remembers*, 11.

p. 122, "Imagine John Lennon . . ." Harry, *The John Lennon Encyclopedia*, 382.

p. 122, "because it is . . ." Coleman, *Lennon, the Definitive Biography,* 563.

p. 123, "It's like the Rome . . ." Henke, *Lennon Legend*, 49.

p. 124, "I'd just arrived . . ." Coleman, *Lennon, the Definitive Biography,* 569.

p. 125, "speak out with . . ." Ibid., 716.

p. 126, "Murderers, rapists . . ." Cott and Doudna, *The Ballad of John and Yoko*, 138.

p. 127, "Success is something . . ." Harry, *The John Lennon Encyclopedia*, 752.

CHAPTER EIGHT: Better and Better

p. 128, "I always was . . ." Sheff, *All We Are Saying*, 158.

p. 128-129, "Yoko and I had . . ." Coleman, *Lennon, the Definitive Biography,* 590.

p. 136, "Yoko knew . . ." Ibid., 593.

p 130 "I know he likes . . ." May Pang and Kenny Edwards, *The Lost Weekend: Living, Loving and Making Rock and Roll,* 5.

p. 130, "The City of . . ." Ibid., 81.

p. 130, "It felt exactly . . ." Coleman, *Lennon, the Definitive Biography,* 596.

p. 131, "Yoko, indeed . . ." Pang and Edwards, *The Lost Weekend: Living, Loving and Making Rock and Roll,* 84.

p. 131, "That's all right," Coleman, *Lennon, the Definitive Biography,* 600.

p 131, "John Lennon has . . ." Goldman, *The Lives of John Lennon*, 493.

p. 132, "I was overwhelmed . . ." Pang and Edwards, *The Lost Weekend: Living, Loving and Making Rock and Roll,* 128.

p. 132, "Musically, my mind . . ." Harry, *The John Lennon Encyclopedia*, 959.

p. 134, "Because it was . . ." Coleman, *Lennon, the Definitive Biography,* 614.

p. 134, "Look what Yoko . . ." Ibid*.,* 615.

p. 134-135, "It's all right wondering . . ." Ibid., 616.

p. 135, "I feel like . . ." Cott and Doudna, *The Ballad of John and Yoko*, 147.

p. 135-136, "I don't want . . ." Goldman, *The Lives of John Lennon*, 556.

p. 136, "Another bloody . . ." Coleman, *Lennon, the Definitive Biography,* 623.

p. 137, "I've always wanted . . ." Sheff, *All We Are Saying*, 61.

p. 137, "Walking away is . . ." Henke, *Lennon Legend*, 55.

p. 137,139, "He didn't come . . ." Harry, *The John Lennon Encyclopedia*, 535.

p. 139, "I'd make two loaves . . ." Sheff, *All We Are Saying*, 5.

p. 139, "Every day . . ." Copy of John Lennon drawing dated 1979.

p. 140, "When John and I . . ." Coleman, *Lennon, the Definitive Biography*, 631.

p. 140, "Only Yoko Ono . . ." Ibid., 633.

p. 140, "Go with it . . ." Ibid., 637.

p. 140-141, "I'm always proud . . ." Sheff, *All We Are Saying*, 56.

p. 141, "Talking about . . ." Ibid., 71.

p. 141, "The house is . . ." "A Love Letter From John And Yoko," *New York Times*, May 27, 1979.

CHAPTER NINE: Dakota Groupies

p. 142, "I was too tight . . ." Goldman, *The Lives of John Lennon*, 654.

p. 143, "Look, here's a song . . ." Ibid.

p. 143, "In the Beatle days . . ." Coleman, *Lennon, the Definitive Biography*, 665.

p. 143, "I kept thinking . . ." Harry, *The John Lennon Encyclopedia*, 104.

p. 144, "I was the real . . ." Sheff, *All We Are Saying*, 70.

p. 144, "Pop stars were . . ." Coleman, *Lennon, the Definitive Biography*, 666.

p. 145, "The whole thing . . ." Harry, *The John Lennon Encyclopedia*, 202.

p. 145, "We have resurrected . . ." Henke, *Lennon Legend*, 58.

p. 146, "an open invitation . . ." Harry, *The John Lennon Encyclopedia*, 593.

p. 146, "When are you going . . ." Sheff, *All We Are Saying*, 30.

p. 146, "I'm going to be . . ." Ibid., 8.

p. 146, "Mahatma Gandhi . . ." Sheff, *All We Are Saying*, 118.

p. 148, "They'll never believe . . ." Harry, *The John Lennon Encyclopedia*, 146.

p. 148, " Do you know . . ." Ibid.

p. 150, "I was devastated . . ." Cott and Doudna, *The Ballad of John and Yoko*, 228.

p. 150, "It is a hard . . ." Harry, *The John Lennon Encyclopedia*, 924.

p. 150, "Daddy, were you . . ." Sheff, *All We Are Saying*, 147

p. 151, "That's how Sean . . ." Coleman, *Lennon, the Definitive Biography*, 684.

p. 151, "I will never recover," Baird, *John Lennon: My Brother*, 162.

p. 151, "It's a drag . . ." Harry, *The John Lennon Encyclopedia*, 587.

p. 152, "it's easier to get . . ." Cott and Doudna, *The Ballad of John and Yoko*, 213.

p. 152, "That was the greatest . . ." Goldman, *The Lives of John Lennon*, 691.

p. 152, "This is not . . ." Cott and Doudna, *The Ballad of John and Yoko*, 207.

p. 152, "People say there is . . ." Ibid.

p. 154, "born out of . . ." Sheff, *All We Are Saying*, 63.

p. 154, "The person that . . ." Denberg, Jody, interview with Julian Lennon, KGSR-FM Radio, June 16, 1999.

p. 155, "He was brilliant . . ." Henke, *Lennon Legend*, 61.

Bibliography

Baird, Julia. *John Lennon: My Brother*. New York:
  Jove Books, 1988.
Coleman, Ray. *Lennon, the Definitive Biography*.
  New York: Harper Perennial, 1985.
Cott, Jonathan, and Christine Doudna. *The Ballad of John
  and Yoko*. Garden City, NY: Dolphin Books,1982.
Cross, Craig. *Beatlesdiscography.com: Day-By-Day/Song-
  By-Song/Record-By-Record*. Lincoln, Nebraska:
  iUniverse, 2004.
Davies, Hunter. *The Beatles*. New York: Dell, 1968.
Goldman, Albert. *The Lives of John Lennon*. New York:
  William Morrow, 1988.
Harry, Bill. *The John Lennon Encyclopedia*. London:
  Virgin Publishing, 2000.
Henke, James. *Lennon Legend*. San Francisco:
  Chronicle Books, 2003.
Henke, James, and Parke Puterbaugh. *I Want to Take You Higher*.
  San Francisco: Chronicle Books, 1997.
Lennon, John, and Yoko Ono. "A Love Letter From John
  And Yoko." *New York Times*, May 27, 1979.
Lennon, Julian. "Interview with Julian Lennon."
  By Jody Denberg. KGSR-FM Radio, June 16, 1999.
Pang, May, and Kenny Edwards. *The Lost Weekend:
  Living, Loving and Making Rock and Roll*. New York:
  SPI Books, 1983.
Sheff, David. *All We Are Saying*. New York: St. Martin's
  Press, 2000.
Shotton, Pete, and Nicholas Schaffner. *John Lennon in My Life*.
Briarcliff Manor, NY: Stein and Day, 1983.
Wenner, Jann. *Lennon Remembers*. London: Verso, 2000.

Web sites

http://www.beatlesdiscography.com
Thorough Web site containing detailed year-by-year
timeline of Beatles history and information about their
songs.

http://www.johnlennon.com
Contains a wide array of information on Lennon and those
closest to him, along with post-Beatle song lyrics and
links to several other Lennon-related sites.

http://www.geocities.com/sara1000a/main01.htm
Unofficial but comprehensive collection of lyrics to all
Beatles songs.

http://www.a-i-u.net
Yoko Ono's official Web site.

http://www.lennon.net
Web site of the "Liverpool" Lennons including Cynthia
and Julian.

http://www.rockhall.com
Web site of the Rock and Roll Hall of Fame and Museum,
including information on inductees (both the Beatles and
John Lennon as a solo artist) and exhibitions.

Index